"There is no dating coach in the c[...] Wygant. His methods work! If you [...] [...]ate or just a healthy happy relationship then this book is a must read."

—Karen Ammond,
President/Publicist, KBC Media Relations

"Throw away the other books; this book is destined to give rise to a new movement, becoming the definitive guide to meeting new people to date."

—Mia Kaminsky,
former casting producer,
Blind Date, Shipmates, Date Patrol,
and Queer Eye for the Straight Guy.

"If you really want to find the love of your life . . . READ THIS BOOK. It's the best I've seen on this topic."

—Karen Grant,
The Karen Grant Show

"I wish I'd read this book before I met my current girlfriend because I'm sure I could have done a lot better." —Jamie Rhonheimer,
coproducer of the CBS sitcom *Yes, Dear.*

"Single people across the country can improve their prospects, and their attitude, with this approach."

—Steven Lefkowitz,
producer, MSNBC

"This book will be a valuable assest . . . David Wygant and Bryan Swerling have done a great deal in this manual to demystify and simplify the daunting task of meeting new people."

—Dr. Steven Phillipson, clinical director,
Center for Cognitive-Behavioral Psychotherapy

"Not only should people read this book who want to learn how to meet new people for relationships, they should read this book on how to network with people in their career . . . David Wygant is a master."

—David Hoffman,
music publishing

"*Always Talk to Strangers* should always be your first stop for real-world dating advice that will take you from self-consciousness to companionship."

—Dan Sandman,
former news producer, NBC Miami

"David Wygant's *Always Talk to Strangers* drives straight to the center of what it takes to meet a new person . . . If you're a real person, looking for real relationships, you won't be let down with this book."

—Peter Coyote,
actor/writer

"As this book makes perfectly clear, before you have your Gracie to say goodnight to, you have to say hello."

—Steven Yesner,
freelance network news producer/writer

Always Talk to Strangers

3 Simple Steps
to Finding the Love of Your Life

david wygant
with bryan swerling

a perigee book

A Perigee Book
Published by the Penguin Group
Penguin Group (USA) Inc.
375 Hudson Street, New York, New York 10014, USA
Penguin Group (Canada), 10 Alcorn Avenue, Toronto, Ontario M4V 3B2, Canada
(a division of Pearson Penguin Canada Inc.)
Penguin Books Ltd., 80 Strand, London WC2R 0RL, England
Penguin Group Ireland, 25 St. Stephen's Green, Dublin 2, Ireland
(a division of Penguin Books Ltd.)
Penguin Group (Australia), 250 Camberwell Road, Camberwell, Victoria 3124, Australia
(a division of Pearson Australia Group Pty. Ltd.)
Penguin Books India Pvt. Ltd., 11 Community Centre, Panchsheel Park, New Delhi—
110 017, India
Penguin Group (NZ), cnr. Airborne and Rosedale Roads, Albany, Auckland 1310, New Zealand
(a division of Pearson New Zealand Ltd.)
Penguin Books (South Africa) (Pty.) Ltd., 24 Sturdee Avenue, Rosebank, Johannesburg 2196,
South Africa
Penguin Books Ltd., Registered Offices: 80 Strand, London WC2R 0RL, England

Copyright © 2005 by Big Man Productions, Inc., and Bryan Swerling
Text design by Kristin del Rosario
Cover design by Ben Gibson

PRINTING HISTORY
Perigee trade paperback edition / March 2005

PERIGEE is a registered trademark of Penguin Group (USA) Inc.
The "P" design is a trademark belonging to Penguin Group (USA) Inc.

Library of Congress Cataloging-in-Publication Information

Wygant, David.
    Always talk to strangers : 3 simple steps to finding the love of your life / David Wygant and
Bryan Swerling. — 1st Perigee pbk. ed.
        p. cm.
    ISBN 0-399-53066-5
    1. Single people—Psychology. 2. Dating (Social customs). 3. Interpersonal attraction.
4. Beauty, Personal. 5. Grooming for men. 6. Fashion. I. Swerling, Bryan. II. Title.

HQ800.W94 2005
646.7'7—dc22   2004055098

PRINTED IN THE UNITED STATES OF AMERICA

10   9   8   7   6   5   4   3

David Wygant would like to dedicate this book to Bryan Swerling for his hard work on bringing David's thoughts and ideas together. Alison Horstmeyer for her love and support, and his favorite client T.G., for all that he's learned through their crazy adventures.

Bryan Swerling would like to dedicate this book to David Wygant for his friendship and the opportunity to collaborate with him, his mother, father, and sister for their love and support, and Jessica Hollander, for her love and many dedicated hours of editorial assistance.

Contents

the carrot girl

One night many years ago, after a trip to the gym, I went into my neighborhood supermarket to buy dinner. As I rounded the corner of the second aisle, I noticed a beautiful woman. When I say beautiful, I don't mean just her body and face. There was something else about her that was even more appealing. Something radiated from her. She lit up the store with her energy. I wasn't the only person who noticed, either. Every man she passed stopped and stared. I followed her through the store, trying to think of some way to approach her.

Never one to be at a loss for words, I suddenly found myself speechless. For the first time since I was a young man, I found myself uncomfortable in my own skin and filled with anxiety. I told myself that I shouldn't bother, that I smelled like sweat, that my hair was graying, that she probably had a boyfriend . . .

When she stopped to look at some carrots, I finally had my chance. Her hands were full, her basket was getting heavy, and she was clearly looking around for one of those plastic bags they keep around the produce section. I rushed over to the nearest roll and pulled one off. I walked right up to her and held it open for her carrots. She looked at me as if I was her knight in shining armor.

"Thank you," she said.

"My pleasure," I mumbled.

Staring at her, I saw my future with this gorgeous creature; I envisioned our engagement, our wedding, kids, a house, even old age. I was acutely aware of all the other men who were staring at me with a mixture of admiration and envy. Meanwhile, I was just standing there, doing nothing at all.

As the seconds passed, our stares slowly became uncomfortable. I was losing the moment and the momentum. I was too busy thinking about the people around me, what she was thinking of me, and about our future together. Her eyes fell to the bag in her hands; she glanced back up, and said, "Have a nice day."

With that, she took her basket, walked over to the cashier, and disappeared.

I stood in that spot for at least five minutes, berating myself. How could I have let her get away and what was I thinking? Quickly, the other men who had been watching went about their business, either relieved or disgusted at my quick demise. Eventually, I finished my shopping, checked out, went home, and sat in front of my television for the rest of the evening, utterly depressed.

I continued to think about her for weeks, and told The Carrot Girl story to everyone I knew. I felt a little bit better when I realized that almost all of them had carrot girls, gas station guys, or someone, somewhere, who had gotten away without even a proper introduction. My regret was happy to have the company.

Three months later, I went to a party at my friend Charlie's house. A half hour after I got there, the door opened. There entered an old acquaintance of mine, Scott, with none other than The Carrot Girl on his arm. My heart dropped into my stomach. When I could speak, I turned to Charlie.

"What's Scott doing with her?" I asked, shocked.

Charlie turned toward the door.

"You mean Vanessa. Oh yeah, isn't she unreal?"

I had to ask.

"When did he meet her?" I managed to squeak.

The answer nearly killed me.

"About two months ago, I think. On the sidewalk in Brentwood," Charlie replied. "He just walked right up to her, told her he thought she was beautiful and introduced himself. Sounded like something you would do."

introduction

Once upon a time, a boy could show his romantic interest in a girl by camping out on her doorstep every night until she caved in and went on a date with him. At the time, this behavior was considered courting. Today, it's called stalking.

In the 1950s and early 60s, dating mainly consisted of milk shakes, drive-in movies, and necking at the "spot." If things went well, a couple got married, the man went to work, and the woman stayed home to raise their children—end of story. Boy, have things changed.

Since the mid-1960s, major changes throughout the world have changed our perceptions and daily behavior. The sexual revolution, women's liberation, the civil rights movement, rock n' roll, the drug culture, political cor-rectness, the advent of computers, and expansive mass media have pervaded our lives. Many young people are staying single longer—giving themselves time to soul search and explore their options. We have become a society more committed to our own happiness and well-being than to the institution of marriage for marriage's sake. Yet, in a matter of only a few years, the key to finding a healthy, long-lasting relationship has become a giant mystery. Now, instead of milk shakes and drive-ins, it's speed dating and sexual harassment. We're in a "brave new world" where how to find our soul mate is the hot topic at the forefront of pop culture. Yet, even with everyone talking, few have come upon the answer.

The proof is in the pudding—the 2000 census reported that there were 82 million single adults in the United States. Within major metropolitan areas such as New York, the majority of the adult population is actually composed of singles. Some of this can be attributed to people enjoying staying single longer. However, statistics show that the majority of people are lonely and anxious about fulfilling that childhood dream of companionship. Marriage rates have dropped to a thirty-year low and more than 50 percent of all marriages now end in divorce.

In the United States alone, singles spend over a billion dollars a year on newspapers, magazines, and Internet personals. Websites such as Yahoo Personals and Lavalife receive millions of hits each month. In addition, there are hundreds of other matchmaking Internet sites which receive millions more. We have self-help books, television shows, movies, courses, seminars, and magazines catering to the single person's plight of finding "the one." It's the information age and the information is everywhere you look. With all this knowledge at singles' fingertips, why are the statistics only getting worse and the scurry becoming more desperate?

My theory—too much bad information. In the changing times and media frenzy, common sense has been lost. We've observed and listened to too many ill-informed people and too few realistic ideas about what a love life should and should not be. With more and more people giving poor and conflicting advice, it's time to get back to the basics.

Getting back to the basics doesn't mean resorting to milk shakes, drive-ins, and young marriage. It means picking up on the idea that the baby boomers started with, the idea of a commitment to well-being and happiness. My philosophy is simple. If you want to find a long-lasting, healthy relationship, then get out of the frenzy. Take your time. Accept that most people need to meet a lot of people before they find the right match for themselves. Then, once you recognize this, learn the right way to meet those people. That's what this book is about. It's me, teaching you the mindset and skills to maintain while embarking on your quest to meet new people to date—and then helping you meet those new people.

You may ask, David, why should I trust you above the others? My answer—the proof is in the pudding. Throughout the years I've literally helped thousands—from everyday people, to celebrities and millionaires—become more comfortable with the dating process. As a result of my specializing in working with clients to transform them in short periods of time, I am the only dating coach in the world that can commission five figure fees for a weekend's worth of work. Some clients have even flown me to countries such as Thailand, Peru, Panama, Colombia, the

Ukraine, England, and Spain. Am I telling you this to brag? No. I'm telling you this because I believe that it's substantial proof of my effectiveness.

One of the most rewarding facets of my job as a coach is that I've been asked by three of the largest online dating sites in the country to become one of their "experts" who answers questions and letters from their users on a wide array of topics ranging from first conversations to first dates. I am currently working with Yahoo! Personals, Lavalife.com, and Date.com where I get to hear from and communicate with many different kinds of people, from all walks of life, from around the country.

I know that you too are aching for answers and I'm going to give them to you by helping you to start from scratch. I'm going to teach you how to proactively go after what you want without using cheap tricks or pick-up lines. I'm going to demystify the process of meeting new people and make it simple, without deception.

If you've read books like *The Rules* and thought the advice given by the authors was the cat's meow, you're in for a rude awakening by reading these chapters. There are no hard and fast "rules" here. What you will get is a lesson in how to build your own confidence, how to start a conversation with another person, how to carry on that conversation in a positive way, and then how to ask them on a date in a straightforward, mature manner.

Everything I teach is common sense. You must forget about all of the bad advice and habits you've picked up over the years. With that said, follow my advice and I promise you will begin meeting new people to date, and the end result will be that you will find the relationship you've always wanted. Be aware, however, that this is not a book about relationships. This book is about taking the first step in the process of building relationships—making contact with new people. Master this first step, give yourself options in an abundant world of people, and there's a good chance that relationships will simply fall into place.

A final note—as you read through this book, you'll notice that for the majority of time, I'm speaking to both sexes simultaneously. The reason—I believe that both men and women should use the same common sense and interpersonal communication skills to go about pursuing dates. Of course, there are some core differences between men and women and how they relate to each other once a relationship starts, but when it comes to meeting new people the challenges are identical. After all, this is the 21st century, and women can and should be every bit as proactive as men when pursuing dates. When you come to a section that specifically addresses either men or women, you might want to read it anyway. Your knowledge is your power. Knowing anything about the opposite sex can only benefit you once you go back out into the world.

I hope you enjoy what you read. All things considered, through this book you'll be getting much of what others have paid me large sums of money to teach them. I've never had a disappointed or dissatisfied client in all my years of coaching people in these skills, and rest assured that you will not be the first. So sit back, take a deep breath, grab a cup of coffee, and get ready to change your life.

preparation—before you leave the house

For everything in life worth achieving, we must first master a process. This is especially true when it comes to seeking potential dates or love interests. I've spent many years of my life developing a process that teaches people like you how to meet other single people. The first step in this process is to prepare you mentally and physically for success.

Before teaching my personal clients a single thing about meeting new people, I spend time helping them think about how they view the world—and how the world views them. First, I reshape their mental outlook. By evaluating the destructive philosophies that are encumbering them from approaching others and getting dates, I'm able to introduce them to the correct positive thought processes. These lessons are continually reinforced each and every time I notice them resorting to their old way of thinking until finally, they no longer think destructively.

After completing their mental makeover, the fun really begins. Nine out of ten of my clients, both male and female, benefit from physical makeovers. A physical makeover, as many of you know from watching television, encompasses personal hygiene, grooming, and fashion. Having lived in some of the most fashion-focused cities in the United States, and been hired on network television to perform makeovers, I have a keen sense of what's hot and what's not. I also have a good idea of what works and what doesn't for various types of people. What looks good on your friend or your favorite celebrity may not look good on you. Therefore, when reading this section, try to step out of your shoes for a moment and be objective—as if you were viewing yourself from someone else's perspective.

Take your time reading through this section. Refer to the checklists I provide at the end of these chapters. Continually remind yourself of what you've learned—your dating philosophies will eventually change and your grooming techniques and fashion sense will become habitual. If you follow the advice in this section, you'll be well on your way to being more attractive to the opposite sex. Consider yourself to be my newest client. Now, let's get to work.

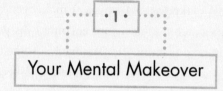

Your Mental Makeover

There are several ways to diminish your chances of meeting new people to date and collaterally, your chances at finding love. But most of the time, the problems involve your mental outlook and not your physicality. I know there are those of you out there who believe that because you may not be the most attractive or the richest of the singles lot, your appeal is severely diminished, but you're wrong! Want proof? Look around you.

Everyday you see people coupled with someone not their financial or physical equal. You see chubby, balding men with thin beautiful women. You see unattractive women with great looking men. Sometimes you'll see a male lawyer who makes tons of money with a female teacher who makes a lot less. Sometimes you'll see a guy who makes very little money whose significant other is a wealthy executive. Why? Because in reality, two elements are essential for long-term intimate relationships—physical chemistry and how two people relate to one another. If those two things work, everything else is based on how well those two people will deal with each other as problems arise through the course of their relationship.

I'll assume that you want to get into a healthy relationship by dating mentally healthy people. To do that, you must be mentally healthy yourself. That means thinking about yourself in a positive way—while being aware of your insecurities. For example, say you're a man who has just been turned down by a woman for a date. Instead of berating yourself as a "loser," instead, try saying to yourself, "I'll never know the real reasons why this woman didn't want to go out with me because I'm not inside of her head. Therefore, I won't register this as a failure, I will register it as a success in that I had the confidence to go after what I wanted and if I keep doing what I'm doing, eventually, a woman who I am attracted to will be responsive."

It's important to stay away from Mental Sound Bytes like "I'm a loser." In these times of mass media, Mental Sound Bytes naturally pop into your head, but ultimately, from a psychological perspective, are damaging, incorrect, and overly simplified ways of how to process information and experience. Think through information and experience before you react. Although you may not change overnight, the more you become aware of this type of negative simplified thinking, the more you will be able to stop and change it as it occurs.

In the following pages, I'm going to address several mental roadblocks, including:

- The "Passive Waiter" Mentality—How the various myths that contribute to this destructive pattern of behavior inhibit your dating experiences.

- Poor Frame of Mind—The elements that not only hold you back from enjoying your singlehood, but also make you unattractive to the opposite sex.

- Awareness and Availability—How to become more aware of the people around you, your body language, and people who you should identify as your potentials.

- Anxiety—How it hinders you in your quest for dates, and techniques to cure it.

the passive waiters

The most common problem with dating today is that a majority of people passively wait for love to fall in their lap. By doing absolutely nothing to increase your chances of getting dates, you actually decrease your chances. It's a numbers game, folks! Unless you're one of the lucky few who have found true love early in life, you have to get out in the game, meet as many people as possible, and play the odds until you find the right one.

We're a society obsessed with our careers and pursuing the American dream. When it comes to our livelihoods, most of us don't sit around waiting for things to happen to us, rather, we make things happen. When you apply for a job, you send out a hundred resumes. You don't send out just one and hope for the best—not if you ever hope to get hired and be successful. Why is it that when it comes to love, so many people believe that it'll someday simply fall out of the sky? It's all a matter of the faulty thinking patterns of The Passive Waiter Mentality.

In the following pages, I will discuss the five myths that contribute to the Passive Waiter Mentality. They are: The Entitlement Myth, The Pop Culture Myth, The Societal Myth, The Tradition Myth, and The Introverted Myth.

THE ENTITLEMENT MYTH

I can't tell you how many clients have come to me and said, "David, you're my last resort. I've done the right things. I've been a good person. Yet, nothing ever happens to me. I never get asked out. I'm alone and I'm tired of being alone. Aren't I entitled to a little happiness?" My response to them is a resounding, "No."

People aren't entitled to happiness. People have to work for happiness just as they have to work for a successful career, and in the very same way they have to work and save for a house, a car, a stereo, retirement, or even to maintain friendships.

When you believe you're entitled to something, you won't go after it. You passively wait around hoping whatever you feel entitled to will be handed to you on a silver platter. When no one serves it up to you, you become angry, upset, and frustrated. "Damn it," you proclaim. "I'm a good person. I do the right things. I'm entitled to this." You become reactive, instead of proactive.

In our daydreams, we'd all like the most important and most difficult to achieve things in our lives to be handed to us. Many of us sit around, look out the window and dream of being famous, admired, rich, and super successful. Yet, in reality, that just doesn't happen to most of us. However, even if it did just happen to us overnight, would we really be able to appreciate it the same way as if we'd strived and worked hard for it? Most likely not. Therefore, it's in the process of striving for something that we find the greatest rewards. We grow by working for something, not just getting it.

You may desire dates and to fall in love, but you're not entitled. You must put effort into finding a mate just like you must work for anything else in life. You'll have to be proactive instead of reactive. You'll have to take chances, move around, explore, open up, go against your natural human instinct to wait for a Prince—or Princess Charming.

Now, some of you may say, "David, I've never felt entitled to love. I've done everything I can to find someone. I've dated hundreds of people, done blind dates, Internet dating, and speed dating. I walk up to people on the street and introduce myself. I've had one relationship after another. Yet, nothing substantial has ever come out of any of it. I'm getting older. I don't feel entitled, I just feel tired and worn down." My response to these people—*keep going!*

In the professional world, some people don't become successful at a career until later in life. If they had stopped pushing for success after some negative experiences, they may never have had the profound impact that they eventually did. For instance, Abraham Lincoln lost more than five elections before he was elected President of the United States and Henry Miller didn't sell his first book until he was in his forties and even then he was broke until late in his life. *Keep going!*

Success happens to each of us at different times in our lives and the same is true when it comes to love. So, don't compare yourself to your friends or the average person your age. You may be forty and still single, while all of your friends are married with kids. However, they may be in unhappy marriages, headed for divorce, or even cheating on their significant others. They may sit around and daydream of the days when they were free to experience the world and actually be jealous of you—despite telling you otherwise. Consistently be aware of negative thoughts and try to look at the big picture.

Start to look at your life as one long journey where there is no timeline as to when significant events must happen to you. Erase the idea that you must go to school in your teens and early twenties, get married in your mid-twenties, have kids in your later twenties and early thirties, build wealth in your forties and fifties, retire in your sixties, and start dying in your seventies. Leave this conventional thinking to the sheep in our society. You may not find the great love of your life until you're sixty—and there's nothing wrong with that.

THE POP CULTURE MYTH

We're bombarded with pop culture. It's next to impossible to go through a single moment of your everyday life without encountering a book, a magazine, television, advertising, music, billboards, movies—and they all send a message about how love is supposed to happen.

D. H. Lawrence once said, ". . . the real trouble about women is that they must always go on trying to adapt themselves to men's theories of women." If Lawrence were alive today, he may reword that bit of wisdom to read, ". . . the real trouble with society is that it must always go on trying to adapt itself to the theories of those few people controlling the media."

The most dangerous theory that the media tries to sell you is that love is fate. Movies like *Serendipity* and *Sleepless in Seattle* play on our hopes that our love is predetermined and written in the stars. Ask yourself how many times you've seen the story lines in those two particular movies happen in real life! Rarely, if ever, right?

Recognize that love is not fate or predetermined. In fact, there isn't just one person in this world that would be a great match for you, there are many. There are over five billion people in the world. Is it realistic to think the preordained one for you just happens to be living in your hometown and that you're meant to meet them between the ages of twenty and twenty-five? No.

Sometimes as an audience, we forget that we're watching escapism. We forget that we're not in a movie and tend to believe that our lives should be like one. Recognize that if you think this way, you're setting yourself up for a disaster.

Don't buy into the myths that Hollywood sells to you for entertainment and allow it to affect your reality. Don't let what you watch on the big or small screen convince you to passively wait for love to fall into your lap. Chances are, it won't. You have to get out there, be proactive, and start meeting new people everyday so you increase your chances of finding someone that you relate to. If you meet the right person, love will develop over time. Your only fate is the fate you create for yourself by being proactive.

THE SOCIETAL MYTH

Have you ever complained to someone you know about your dating life and they try to console you by saying, "Oh, honey. Don't worry. It'll happen. The right person will come along when you least expect it. That's how I met my spouse."

For the majority of us, the right person will come along when we least expect it, but not before we've worked to find them. Some people are lucky—they marry their high school or college sweethearts and live happily ever after. The majority of us aren't that lucky. Yet, there's nothing wrong with having to work a little bit harder or wait a little bit longer to find the right one. As I said before, when they do come along, it will make you appreciate them even more.

Personally, when someone I knew in a relationship used to say to me, "It will come along when you least expect it," I got annoyed. People mean well when saying it, but it's also condescending and doesn't make you feel any better about your current state of loneliness. Perhaps this can make you feel better; the majority of people, your family, friends, and coworkers know nothing more about love or finding it than you do. Again, many people get lucky at a young age, many people have worked harder at finding love than they lead you to believe, and many people may not be as complicated and sophisticated as you— they may have settled for the first person who came along who was attentive to their needs.

When it comes to the societal myth, my advice is simple. If certain friends, family, and coworkers of yours don't understand the concept of proactive dating, then don't talk to them about your dating life. It will only serve to frustrate you. When you need a boost, either reread this book or call upon people who relate to your current situation. It'll make you feel better to know that you have people to lean on who have the same objectives.

THE TRADITION MYTH

Many women believe that men are always supposed to make the first move and that it's a man's responsibility to do the courting. Books like *The Rules* teach women how to play men with regard to this tradition. It's trickery and it's unhealthy. Women must stop buying into this deceptive nonsense on how to draw men to them by playing games.

It's the year 2005. Women run large corporations, governments, are successful doctors and lawyers, and are highly paid movie stars. If women have become assertive in their careers, why do they fear the same sense of empowerment when it comes to men? Most of the time I believe they're simply afraid they'll scare men off or be perceived as "loose." The fact is, if you scare a man for starting a conversation with him and asking to get together sometime, he's the wrong man for you anyway. You don't have to live your life playing to the backward thinking of men who aren't evolved.

Men, if a woman approaches you, be flattered and thank your lucky stars that for once in your life you didn't have to make the first move. Women, go after what you want. Get out there and get in the ballgame. Don't spend your life passively waiting for men to approach you. If you see someone you want, go after them.

THE INTROVERT MYTH

Introverted people develop shyness from an early age—it's every bit as much of their personality to keep to themselves as it is for an extrovert to be the life of the party. Introverts are nonaggressive in most areas of their lives, not just when it comes to dating.

Unfortunately, most introverts, because of their shyness, become wallflowers. In the world of dating, this translates into their taking what they can get. Rarely, if ever, would an introvert see someone they were interested in and approach that person. Instead, they stand around like magnets, hoping that someone will be attracted to them and make the first move. They're condemned to a self-imposed prison where they wait around and simply hope that they get a great cellmate.

Being introverted is a crutch that timid people rely on to stay within their safety zones. "I can't approach people. I'm too shy," they say. It's a myth that introverts can't be more proactive in their quest to find dates or love.

To introverts, the very thought of approaching a new person is anxiety provoking. What introverts don't realize is that it doesn't have to be that way. Just because you've had problems meeting people in the past doesn't mean you won't have new opportunities. One of the reasons you may feel so much anxiety is that no one ever taught you how to approach people in a creative, nonaggressive way.

As I teach later in this book, just by learning how to nonchalantly start a conversation with another person of the opposite sex, you will feel more comfortable. Introverts especially should read the chapter in this book entitled The Indirect Approach. Also, there are great techniques I've developed for introverts, such as Boot Camp Internet Dating, which will also help to overcome their anxiety. Shyness is no longer an excuse to passively wait around!

Don't buy into the myths that say that love will fall into your lap, that there's only one person out there for you, that men should always make the first move, or that you're too shy to meet anyone. Instead, rid your mind of them, and if they start to creep back, keep pushing them down. Why be a passive waiter and condemn yourself to a life of missed opportunities? *You* do the selecting. Love will happen when you least expect it, but don't expect love to just happen. Give it a push.

poor frame of mind

Now that you are no longer a passive waiter, I'd like to address another problem that may be affecting your chances of finding dates and as a result, love. This section has nothing to do with waiting around for companionship and has everything to do with how you relate to yourself and to your potential companions.

In this section, I'll address the characteristics of someone with a Poor Self-Image, Poor Outlook, Poor Partner Philosophy, as well as someone who puts undue pressure upon themselves to succeed in the dating world. I'll explore how all of these traits, either alone or cumulatively, can hurt your chances for success in the world of dating.

POOR SELF-IMAGE

Everyone has an image of themselves—what's yours? Overall, do you like yourself? Are you patient with your shortcomings? Or are you brutally harsh with your inadequacies? Are you upbeat and positive? Or are you always down, negative, and complaining? Of course, not everyone is positive all the time, and not everyone is negative all the time. However, on the whole, most people fall into one category or another. Think about the people in your life and sort them by who is more positive than negative and vice versa. Who do you enjoy spending time with the most?

Your self-image begins developing in early childhood and carries on throughout the rest of your life. If you're like most people and had a hard time as a child and haven't gotten over it, now is the time to start the healing process. Many adults still tend to look in the mirror and see themselves at ten, rather than as the adult they are in the present. If at ten you were overweight or picked upon, or didn't fit in for some reason, you must learn to see yourself as you are now and not as you were then. For an example, take a former client of mine named Robert.

Robert was a millionaire and a successful entrepreneur. He wasn't handsome, but he wasn't ugly either. Given the right frame of mind, he had the ability to attract many women. However, Robert was once a chubby, pimply-faced teenager who never fit in, and was relentlessly picked on in his younger years. Despite Robert's education, hard work, travel experience, and sophistication, he still saw himself as that ten-year-old boy. As a result, he didn't think he was good enough for any woman.

Perhaps you're like Robert and have a poor self-image. If

that's the case, work on being nice to yourself and really evaluate how far you've come in life since those early days. If you think about it, you'll be amazed. See yourself as the person you are in the present, not the person from the past. Remember, as children and teenagers, we have very little control over how the world around us relates to and accepts us. We simply haven't built up the awareness and skills that are required to take more control over our environment. In a way, children are victims of their own childhood. But, you're no longer a victim. You are in complete and total charge of your life now. Confidence is an alluring scent and people love to smell it. Don't let *you* beat *you* before you've even started!

POOR OUTLOOK

Closely related to having a poor self-image is having a Poor Outlook on the world. There's a dramatic difference between people who look at the glass as half empty or half full. People who are constantly lamenting about the world and their lot in life are frustrating to be around and often repel company, instead of drawing it in. If those people are lucky, they'll sometimes draw other complainers into their social circle so they can commiserate together.

How often do you complain about your career, your family, your friends, your lovers or past lovers? If you answer, "a lot," then it's time you stop. Get a new outlook—a fresh one, a positive one.

Buddhists say that much of life is painful and that the sooner you accept it, the sooner you'll be on the road to happiness. The truth is, life is an uphill battle. Deal with it. Learn to laugh about it. Don't fight it. If you keep a positive attitude and have a good outlook on life, perhaps you'll find someone else out there who does also—someone you can weather the storm with. If you must complain, use it to your advantage—be comedic about it. You can even be self-deprecating. However, rarely should you complain in mixed company and never should you complain when you first meet a new person.

POOR PARTNER PHILOSOPHY

A Poor Partner Philosophy is a skewed view of what we think other people should be. The two main categories of people with poor partner philosophies are the Rigid List People and the Narcissists.

Rigid List People are those of you out there who have a list a mile long of qualifications a person must meet before you date them. Most of the time, unless you're set up on a blind date or have information on someone from their Internet dating profile, you won't know someone's qualifications from the outset. Most of the time you'll only be presented with a physical image. I suggest you give everyone you meet a chance. I don't care if you're a supermodel and a short bald guy with excessive body hair asks you out. You should go out with him. He may have a great personality and you may quickly forget about his looks.

Moreover, you should immediately stop putting so much emphasis on others' careers. That goes for both men and women. Women—not every man you meet has to be a professional. If someone is a nonprofessional, you should go out with him. Men—stop being scared of successful women. If a woman is the

CEO of a *Fortune* 500 company, you should embrace the opportunity to learn from her. Get rid of your hangups. Give everyone a chance and I guarantee that you'll be headed for change.

The second type of Poor Partner Philosophy applies to narcissists. Narcissism is a commonly misunderstood personality disorder where the narcissist is mistaken for someone who is vain and in love with themselves. In actuality, narcissists are always trying to get the people around them to love them.

Narcissists are constantly in need of other people's approval. One way this affects dating and relationships is that narcissists need to have their friends and family be impressed by whomever they are seeing. Sometimes, this will manifest itself in a man needing to be with a beautiful woman so that all of his friends will think he's special. At other times, this will manifest itself in a woman needing to be with a man who has the most amazing job in the world so that her friends envy the catch she has made for herself. If this is you, you need to stop immediately.

Realize that the people you date aren't a direct reflection of you. In a way they may represent you, but they shouldn't substantiate you as a person. A narcissist wants their peers' approval, and after all the adulation is gone they're left with the person, and must then deal with the consequences of that relationship.

A good way to determine if you have this problem is to gauge how you feel when you're dating someone and you bring them around your friends. See how badly you want to know what they think of your new love interest. Think about whether or not you find yourself wondering what they're thinking. If you do, don't ask them. Just ride out the storm. If they say something about that person without being asked first, then you may respond.

Say, "He/she is pretty smart" or "Yeah, he/she has a great job."
But, don't wait for their approval and certainly don't seek it.

PRESSURE

Have you ever seen the movie *My Cousin Vinny*? One of the
funniest scenes in the film is when Marisa Tomei is standing on
the front porch, stomping her foot, and yelling at Vinny about
how her "Biological clock is ticking like *this* . . ." In reality,
women do tend to take their biological clock very seriously.

Most women, from an early age, dream of getting married and
having children. Unlike men, their chances of this decrease as the
years go by. Despite a new generation of *Sex and the City*–type
women who aren't rushing into commitments, most women still
would like to be settled down by age thirty. Unfortunately, when
this doesn't happen, many go into freak-out mode, constantly
droning on the question of whether they will be able to fulfill
their dreams of having a family. As a result of this self-imposed
pressure, women can seriously hurt their chances of ever meeting a man to fall in love with, much less having children. Here's
an example:

Several years ago I met a woman named Rachel. Rachel was
in her early thirties. She was stunningly beautiful and I couldn't
wait to take her on a date. One night we went out, had a great
time, and concluded the date with a kiss in front of her doorstep.
My heart was racing. I really liked her and couldn't wait to take
her out again.

The following week, I asked her out again for a Saturday
night. She told me that she had a Christmas party to attend on
the Upper West Side of Manhattan, but that I should pick her up

at eleven that evening and we'd go out for drinks afterwards. At eleven I waited in a taxi in front of the address she gave me, anxious to see the woman I'd been dreaming about all week long. When she got in the cab, her demeanor was completely different than the previous week. She was quiet and pensive, staring out the window. Suddenly, I felt uncomfortable. I asked her if she was okay and she replied, "No."

When we got to the lounge to have drinks, I asked her if she wanted to talk about what was bothering her. "That party I just came from," she said to me. "That was my best friend's party. She's married to this great guy and has two beautiful kids and has this perfect house." I sat back. "So what's the problem?" I asked. "The problem is, all of my friends are married and are having kids. I'm thirty-three-years old. I'm not even close. I don't understand why this is happening to me," she said sadly, tears in her eyes. "I mean, I was the pretty one. I was the one with all the boyfriends. And now, even if I met someone today and got engaged and married within the year, I would be at least thirty-five or thirty-six before I could have kids. And what are the chances of that even happening?" With that, she broke out into a full cry.

Needless to say, I was in a bad situation. First, a girl that I really liked had just starting crying to me about her lot in life. Second, we were only on a second date. Third, as a man, I couldn't relate to her biological-clock problem, although it seemed her issues ran even deeper than just that. Fourth, she had showed me how much pressure she was putting on herself to be like everyone else and was obviously very uncomfortable with where she was at that point in time—very unattractive qualities.

Despite her outburst, I did my best to console her. I tried to talk to her and explain that she was a beautiful, intelligent, so-phisticated woman, and that good things were in store for her if she would just be patient. With that, she had a sudden realization of what she'd just done in front of me, and asked me to pay the bill so she could go home.

Later that week, I phoned Rachel to see how she was doing. She told me that she didn't think it was a good idea if we saw each other again—that in fact, she was done dating for awhile until she got her head on straight. I assured her that she had nothing to be embarrassed about and that we could try to start over—but in her mind, the damage had been done. She had revealed too much, too soon. In a way, she was right. Despite my willingness to move on from the situation, I would never see Rachel again as the confident person I saw that first night. Pressure destroys confidence in oneself and confidence in where one is in their life. Everyone has insecurities here and there, but what's more important than what those insecurities are, is how you deal with them.

In the end, I was devastated that Rachel was not more skilled with her emotions. Up to that point in my life, I had rarely if ever had a first date with someone where afterward I felt there was so much potential for a long-term relationship. Without reservation, I can say that had she been more comfortable with who she was and where she was, that something serious could have developed between us. Who knows, perhaps with me, she would have found the answer to what was ailing her. Of course, we never had the chance to find out.

If you're a woman whose biological clock is ticking and hav-ing a family comes up in conversation, say, "Sure, I'd like to have a family someday. If it happens, it happens. If it doesn't, it doesn't. What's more important to me is finding someone to share my life with." Ask yourself, what sounds more appealing to you—the example I just gave, or how Rachel approached it? Need I say more?

Of course, women with ticking biological clocks are only one example of how pressure can affect your ability to date and develop relationships. Perhaps you are a twenty-eight-year-old male whose parents are constantly pestering you about getting married and how much they want grandchildren. Maybe you're a fifty-year-old divorcee who is afraid of growing old alone, or a person of any age who has traditionally not fared well on the dating scene and looks at every person they approach and get a date with as if it'll be their last.

I once had a client named Jack. Jack was thirty years old and approaching that time in his life where he really wanted to settle down with a woman. However, life threw him a curve ball. After eight years of working with the same company, Jack got laid off. After being unemployed for a year, Jack was forced to give up his apartment and temporarily move back in with his parents until he could come up with some kind of plan to get his career back on track. He was putting himself under a tremendous amount of pressure. After all, his friends were growing more financially secure by the day. They were buying houses, getting married, and many were even having children.

Over the years, Jack, like many people, had defined himself by his career and his possessions. He'd let those things substantiate him as a person and used them to his advantage with members of the opposite sex. Now that he no longer had those things, he was convinced that no woman would ever want to talk to him until he regained what he had lost.

One day, Jack approached me, told me his story, and then explained that he was considering going back to school, but wasn't sure yet. He then emphasized that he was scared that if he met a woman and the inevitable conversation came up regarding his career and living accommodations, that revealing the truth would cause her to go running out the door. My first response was, "What's so bad about being thirty and going through a change of life? Where is it written that you have to be just like your friends and that your future has to be spelled out?"

Jack stared at me without an answer. He was speechless. "When you go out and start a conversation with a woman you're attracted to, if it comes up, don't try to hide your predicament, embrace it. Use it to your advantage," I said. "Take the pressure off yourself. Allow yourself to just be comfortable with who you are and where you are at this moment in your life. And at this moment of your life, you're in limbo. So what?"

"So if a woman asks me what I do, what exactly should I say?" Jack asked. "Say you worked for a company for eight years, you got laid off, you've been having trouble finding a position suitable to your skills and needs, and you're contemplating going back to get your MBA so you can get a leg up on the competition. That you are currently applying to schools and when the time comes to make a decision, you'll cross that bridge. In the meantime, you're still looking around for work, you have some free time, and you'd like to take her out for drinks sometime." Jack smiled at me, "Is it really that easy?" he asked. "Yes," I said. "Just being comfortable with where you are in life and who you are is 90 percent of the battle."

Later that day, Jack went out to a coffee shop, sat down, and was reading through a book about MBA programs. He struck up a conversation with a woman sitting at the table next to him. She was about his age and a lawyer. Had Jack tried to cover up, he would have blown the opportunity. However, when they began talking, the woman thought it was great that he was so cool and positive, and they went out later that night.

In any form, pressure acts as human repellent. It flashes across your forehead like a big neon sign and tells potential companions to keep moving on. So what's the answer? It's exactly as I told Jack—become comfortable with who you are and where you are in your life. Your quest to pursue dates, a relationship, or anything must be seen as a journey—your own personal journey where you learn about yourself, people, and the world around you. Your only obligation during this journey is to yourself, not to your friends, not to your family, and not to society. Never let outside sources dictate how you feel about you. If someone around you is applying pressure and it is making you uncomfortable, sit down with them, and ask them nicely to stop. Tell them that it's creating a rift in your relationship. If the pressure you feel is coming from within you, give yourself permission to go on the adventure without knowing where it may lead. Embrace the uncertainty that is life.

availability and awareness

Up until now, we have mainly evaluated negative, unproductive thinking and how that can affect your chances of obtaining dates and, eventually, relationships. Here, I'll address two issues that have less to do with thought and more to do with lack of thought—obliviousness.

We live in a busy world where most of us are running around all day long trying to meet goals. All of us, to some extent, wake up in the morning with a checklist of what we want and hope to accomplish during that day. Most of us are on autopilot from the moment we leave our homes in the morning until the moment we walk back in the door in the evening.

Many of you out there may be going through life in a daze. The result—you're either unavailable for people around you to approach you or you're unaware of opportunities to meet people. Perhaps, even both. The following two sections address your availability and your awareness, and how to stay within the present moment so that opportunities do not pass you by.

AVAILABILITY

Imagine that your boss gives you an all-expenses-paid vacation for one week. You get to choose your destination. You go to a travel agent and ask her to see some brochures for vacation spots that fall within your boss's predetermined budget. The agent hands you two brochures. Inside each are several pictures of the vacation spots.

The first one displays photographs of a sunny blue sky, a sandy beach, beautiful ocean water, tan people walking around in shorts, and palm trees. The second one displays photos of a gray sky, rough waters, and people walking around in heavy coats, freezing half to death. Where are you going to go?

The majority of you will have answered the sunny beach. It's inviting, it's relaxing, and it's soothing to the nerves. After all, this is your vacation and you want to enjoy it, not sit in a rainstorm covering up for warmth. Now, imagine that two people have the same characteristics as the photographs you viewed for your vacation. One person is warm and open; the other is cold and scary looking. Which one would you choose to approach?

Well, unless you're an absolute masochist, most people would choose to approach the warm and open person. Warm and open people are inviting, relaxing, and soothing to the nerves just like the beach. Hey, life is tough enough, why would anyone want to complicate things more by hooking up with a hurricane? The lesson: Be available, be the warm open person, and you will be approached.

Projecting a lack of availability can afflict you during your day, as you do your errands, and during work. Most of the time during the course of a day, your unavailability is unintentional and the product of stress. You can actually get so caught up in what you're doing that you emit a frightening vibe to others. Other times during the day, you're simply just too absorbed in your own life to think about smiling and opening up. You may enjoy listening to your music or talking on your cell phone while having coffee or commuting to work, but just remember that no one will approach you because you appear to be otherwise involved. If you must do those things, although I don't re-commend it, then make up for it in other ways, at other times of the day. For example, tomorrow, on your way to work, remind yourself to smile more, relax your shoulders when they get tense, and to become more available to others by looking around. In the Meeting People About Town chapter of this book, I will show you how this can pay off.

Projecting a lack of availability at night can also afflict your evening, as you go out by yourself, or with your friends to social-ize. Many times at night your appearing aloof and unavailable is intentional. If you've ever been out to a popular bar, then you know what I'm talking about. What you see when you walk in the door is a bunch of people standing around putting on their best/worst attitude. Interestingly, almost everyone who goes to a hot bar or club is looking to meet another person, but when they get there, they completely shut down and put up barriers. This is one of the reasons I dislike bars so much for meeting new people. While I'm sure that the people in these hot spots aren't that miserable looking all the time, they seem to think it goes with the territory—how stupid. Why would you go out and spend lots of money in a place just to stand around, look miserable, and meet no one?

Whether your projecting a lack of availability is unintentional or intentional, just understand that anytime you appear unavailable, distant, or preoccupied, people who may normally approach you will not, and you're missing many opportunities to meet a potential date. Keep reminding yourself to smile, and use your eyes to flirt. Give off signs that you're an available person. It works!

AWARENESS

A similar and related problem to appearing unavailable is lack of awareness. When you walk through life in a daze, not only do you miss the beauty of life, but you also miss opportunities to meet new people everywhere. You not only miss their entire presence, but you also miss the signs they're giving you.

When I work with my clients, I teach them observation skills. I have them take notice of anything and everything around them—especially people. First, I teach them to always keep one eye on their surroundings to see who is available for an approach. Second, I teach them to become more aware of people's body language, how they carry themselves, and what they're doing. Third, I have them take note of how people interact with them.

The next time you leave the house, I want you to be really aware of your surroundings. You may think that you always are, but this time I want you to be extra aware. Always keep one eye on what you're doing and one eye on what's going on around you. Look for members of the opposite sex everywhere you go— bookstores, coffee shops, restaurants, movies, etc. A potential date could be the person standing next to you on line to get coffee or the person standing behind the counter serving it. Look around.

Become aware of people looking at you. My clients consistently tell me that they can't tell whether or not people of the opposite sex are looking at them or looking past them. Some clients have told me that they can't figure out if someone is looking at them because they're attractive or unattractive. Chances are if they're looking at you, it's not because you're unattractive. The truth is that people look at things that interest them. If you find people looking at you, then most likely they're interested in something about your appearance. It could be your hair, your eyes, your body, or that you have an interesting face. You may have an interesting energy or presence about you. Be aware of whose eyes are drawn in your direction.

Next, I want you to start studying and becoming aware of people's behavior. Observe their body movements, watch how they interact with others, and then try to figure out what they're thinking. For instance, if you're on a subway, look around and study the faces of the people riding with you. Try to figure out their background, where they've just come from, and where they may be going. Try to figure out their age, if they have a college education, or a master's degree. Pay attention to their clothing, what they're reading, and the way they style their hair. Examine whether or not they dress well or if they seem to have taken excessive time or no time prepping themselves in the morning. Try to place what socioeconomic background they may come from. Ask yourself if you think they seemed rushed. And if you happen to observe someone having a conversation with someone else, pay attention to their eyes. Are they shifting? Do they look bored? Do you think they'd rather be somewhere else or are they enjoying themselves?

The purpose of this exercise is not to have you become a mind reader in a circus. The purpose is to get you to concentrate and get in tune with people you don't know, so that you'll become that much better with people you do know or are trying to get to know.

Last, I want you to be aware of how you interact with people. Do you make people feel comfortable or uncomfortable? Do you feel like people are thrilled to talk to you or do you feel they'd rather be somewhere else? Do you feel like they're simply trying to appease you when they talk to you? How does your sense of humor affect others? Do people say that your humor is over the top? Do people say that you're a nice person? Do people say you have a nice smile or that you have a nice smile and you should smile more? Pay attention to how people are responding to your presence in the world. Are they hostile, are they timid, or are they at ease? Try to figure out your presence for yourself. If you can't, ask someone.

Here's an example: I once had a client named Tony. For years he never knew how powerful and overwhelming his presence was. When he walked into a room, the energy changed before he even opened his mouth. And when he did open his mouth, he had a very deep voice. Unfortunately, Tony didn't know that when he got excited in conversation it could become overwhelming to others around him—he was like a tank driving through a crowd of people. After I worked with Tony, I made him understand that he'd have to take extra-careful steps to tone himself down. It wasn't his fault. He thought he was just being himself—and he was. But unfortunately, he wasn't aware of the power of his presence. Now, when speaking, he makes sure that he speaks more calmly and less passionately, and notices people responding to him more positively. The funny thing is, he still comes across as passionate, just in a less threatening way. How can you adjust who you are? Is your presence hard or soft? Could you turn it up or tone it down? The point here is to be more self-aware of who you are and how others view you, not to give yourself a complete overhaul.

anxiety

There are two types of fear: Real Fear and Fake Fear. Real Fear is being chased through the jungle by a lion that hasn't eaten in a month. Fake Fear is starting a conversation with a stranger. Yet, both fears, whether real or fake, produce anxiety in people.

When getting chased through the jungle, anxiety produces adrenaline and can save your life. When having to start a conversation with a stranger, anxiety can cause you to freeze in your tracks. The result—you miss out on meeting a potential date.

What causes this Fake Fear that in turn produces anxiety is specific to the person suffering it. Some people have a fear of rejection, some people feel they must look perfect before talking to others, some people don't feel they're good enough, and some people are scared of general social situations. Really, the causes are innumerable. Sit back for a moment and think about what goes through your mind when you see someone attractive on the street who you'd like to approach. What stops you? What makes you scared? How does your body react? What thoughts start racing through your mind?

Whatever comes to your mind, write it down and look at it. When you read it, you'll start to realize how silly these little thoughts are. It's as if the old adage our parents told us when we were kids, "never talk to strangers," continues to haunt us in a different form as adults. You have to realize that people are just people. They get up in the morning just like you, they shower, put their clothes on, daydream, work, sleep, and get up the next morning to do it all over again. Stop being afraid of them and *always* talk to strangers.

People have conversations all day long and meet new people all the time. You can be one of them. However, you first have to stop overanalyzing each encounter as if the outcome were a matter of life and death. It isn't. It's just a conversation. The whole art of picking people up has been built up way too much. In truth, the art of picking someone up is essentially the art of starting a conversation with a stranger. You don't have to be the social equivalent of a Picasso to succeed at it. You just have to have people skills—or as I like to say, interpersonal communication skills. You have to learn the right way to start a conversation, the right things to say, the right questions to ask, and know the right time to make your exit. It's that simple. There's nothing to feel anxious about. Later, in Step Three, I'll show you how to do all of this.

There are several key ways to get rid of anxiety:

1. **Be prepared.** Perhaps one of the reasons you get anxious when you're about to approach someone is that you never properly learned the right way to do it and the right things to say. If you were to face Mike Tyson in a boxing match and you were not a trained boxer, naturally you would feel anxious. Consider this book as your training guide to prepare you for your bouts around town. It will give you the tools you need to succeed.

2. **Don't let the outcome substantiate who you are as a person.** For example, if you were to approach a potential date, only to get rebuffed, what's that saying about you as a person? The answer—nothing at all. It's only saying something didn't click. Even if you did something terribly wrong in the process of the approach, it still doesn't mean you're a bad person. It just means that you maybe weren't skilled enough to make it work on that one encounter. It may have nothing to do with you at all. Either way, it doesn't mean that you won't be successful in future encounters. Take note—one person is only one person. There are many more.

3. **The drama is in your own mind.** When we face new and challenging obstacles, we naturally feel a tremendous amount of stress. Sometimes we forget that while we're undergoing that drama, the rest of the world is going about their lives. Remember to take a look around you when you get anxious and see that there's really no big deal. The big deal is in your head. No one else cares. If you approach someone, it's not going to end up in *The New York Times* for everyone to read.

4. **Stop thinking that you have to be perfect.** You don't. If you're the type of person who won't approach someone because you don't look your best or you're not feeling your best, then you're letting far too many opportunities pass you by. As I've said before, life can be an uphill battle, and much of our day is spent dealing with stress and not looking completely put together. That doesn't mean you have to close yourself off from potential opportunities. Don't let your need to be perfect make you anxious about approaching people. It's a waste of energy.

5. **Relax!** Take a deep breath. Get into a Vacation Mentality— that indescribable feeling that overtakes you when arriving at the beach in the Bahamas or in Europe on vacation. You're relaxed, you're open to anything and your fears melt away. We've all had this indescribable feeling at one time or another. As a result, many of us have even met a special someone on that vacation—and with ease. Have you ever wondered why we all hate leaving a nice vacation so much? It's not just because we have to return to work and paying the bills. It's that we are at our best on vaca-

tion. We're real people, relaxed, open to adventure and love. It's only when we get back into the reality of our everyday routine that we change back to our societal-conditioned and closed-off selves. Take some time and meditate. Think back to how you felt on a favorite vacation. Tap into that and then attempt to bring a little piece of it into your everyday life.

6. **Act quickly.** Don't give yourself time to get anxious. I call this the Three-Second Principle. That is, when you see someone you want to meet, move in quickly, within three seconds, before your mind talks you out of it. Don't give your mind time to play tricks on you. Get into the habit of identifying opportunities and moving in almost as soon as you find a target. It'll take some practice, but you'll eventually find that the best way to take control of your anxiety is to never let it out of its cage in the first place.

7. **Set Goals.** People always want to succeed. You don't have to win every time you're out there though. Sure, Rocky would have liked to have won the championship of the world, but what he really wanted was to go out there and show that he could put up a good fight. He just wanted to go the distance. You don't always have to get the phone number or even get a second date. Start with small goals. For example, try to meet three new people a week. Talk to people who are nonthreatening to you. Then, eventually build up to your dream companion types. Your anxiety will decrease with every person you practice on and your skills will improve. Eventually, they'll become second nature. The point is, you should always try to go the distance, one

step at a time. And I promise you that if you continue to apply the principles in this book, every time you go the distance, you'll get better and better.

concluding your mental makeover

What you've just read should give you some insight into the issues that may be affecting your chances of meeting new people to date. Always remind yourself that meeting new people is no trick—it's simple interpersonal communication skills at work. You have them. We all have them. You just need to hone them so you can approach strangers. Rid yourself of the mental roadblocks and you'll be well on your way to meeting someone new. On a piece of paper, write down the ten basic concepts listed on the next page and carry them around in your wallet.

CHECKLIST

- I will not be a passive waiter. I'm not entitled to love, I must work for it. Further, I will not buy into the myths that pop culture, society, or tradition have purported.

- I will be proactive in my social life. Only then, once I'm proactive, will I start to reap the rewards I seek.

- I will have a positive self-image. I'm an accomplished and successful adult.

- I will have a positive outlook on life. People who are positive are more fun to be around.

- I will give everyone a chance. Worst-case scenario, if it doesn't work out, I will learn something new about myself and the world I am a part of.

- I will not seek reassurance from my friends and family. This is my journey, not theirs.

- I am under no pressure to find "the one." Dating is an expedition and I'm going to enjoy the adventure, no matter what it may bring.

- I will be comfortable with who I am and where I am. If there is something I wish to change, I will do it in a positive, proactive manner, and not be a victim.

- I will become more available to people and will become more aware of the world around me. I will pay careful attention to how people may perceive me.

- I will not let Fake Fear and anxiety stop me from getting what I want within my social life. I will set goals. I will relax, act swiftly, and always remember that if I do not venture, I will not gain.

·2·

Your Physical Makeover

Now that we've taken a look inward, let's take a look out. This chapter is designed to enhance and maximize your chances of physically attracting members of the opposite sex. Remember, you don't have to look like Brad Pitt or Julia Roberts to be successful on the dating scene, however, it does help to know what is and what's not attractive.

We've all watched makeover shows and been wowed by the dramatic changes people make after working with professionals. Part of my job as a "dating guru" is to act as an image consultant. In addition to helping people change their negative thinking and teaching them interpersonal communication skills, I help them improve their appearances. Some of you may have even seen me do this on the MTV show *Made*. My challenge for the episode was a worst-case scenario MTV selected named Tony.

When I met Tony, he was an absolute mess. His hair was unkempt and greasy; he had pimples on his face, thick glasses, chapped lips, and yellow teeth. He wore jeans that were three sizes too big for him, dirty sneakers, and a calculator watch. He was tall and lanky with no muscle on his frame whatsoever. Tony was a mix of Lewis, Gilbert, and Booger from the movie *Revenge of the Nerds*. However, at the end of our three weeks working together, he was a new man. Aside from his lankiness, which takes some time to change, everything else was an easy fix.

In addition to Tony having a poor self-image and overall mental outlook, he didn't take care of himself. It was easy to see why Tony repelled women. Beauty may be in the eye of the beholder, but there's still a general and basic set of criteria for personal hygiene, fashion, and grooming that most of us adhere to. Those who don't follow these basic criteria generally find themselves left out in the cold or with people equally slovenly as themselves. You don't have to be rich to look good. You just have to be creative, and have the motivation to seek help.

Chances are you're not as bad as Tony, but if you're unsure of what looks good, open your eyes and turn on the television to the E! Entertainment channel, or *Access Hollywood*. Go to the newsstand and buy magazines like *GQ, Vogue, Vanity Fair, Cosmopolitan, Lucky,* and *Maxim*. You can emulate a lot of the looks on the pages without spending too much money.

On the following pages, I'm going to give you the quickest and easiest ways to make yourself more attractive to the opposite sex. I'll address body fat, personal hygiene, grooming, and fashion. Sometimes, I'll be addressing both men and women at the same time; other times, I'll address the sexes separately. As I said in the beginning of the book, men and women don't have to read sections of the book specifically designed for the other sex. However, it doesn't hurt to brush up on what each gender has to go through to look good. It's knowledge that you can always use when you first meet someone or when you're on a date.

fit or fat

Don't worry, I'm not going to make you feel even worse about your body than you may already feel. Pop culture does enough of that to all of us. Brad Pitt and Julia Roberts are thrust in front of our faces everyday, leaving us to think that we need to have their bodies to succeed at dating. Not true! You don't have to have ripped abs or the perfect butt to meet people to date. While it doesn't hurt, it probably won't make or break any opportunities for you. Many people I know with a spare tire around their middle aren't only great at meeting new people to date, but many have ended up in happy, successful relationships, sometimes even with people who are in much better shape than themselves.

However, it never hurts to get in shape. Not only for the obvious reason that as we get older, a healthful lifestyle leads to longevity and can prevent future physical illness, but also because it makes you feel good to exercise. Achieving a healthy body gives you confidence by making you look better in your clothes and by giving you more energy.

Join a gym. If you can afford it, get a personal trainer. Do whatever it takes to motivate yourself. Hate the idea of a gym and envision yourself running on the treadmill like a rat on a wheel? There's a solution: Get out there and start finding alternative ways to get some exercise. Buy a bicycle. Do yoga. Walk.

Run. Bowl. Do something. Work those muscles now while you're still young enough to do it. Anywhere you pursue a healthy body, you'll find other singles. Later, in the Meeting People About Town chapter of this book, I'll list some of the best places to get exercise and meet new people to date.

In addition to exercise, you must maintain a healthy diet. Many of you have struggled with your weight for years by going on yo-yo diets and following the latest crash diet fads. I understand your pain—it's tough. However, if you take care of your body, your body will take care of you in return.

Take a Sunday afternoon to explore your local supermarket. Perhaps even pick up one of the new healthy-lifestyle guides at your local bookstore and begin to make some serious nutritional changes in your daily diet. I guarantee you that the choices you make every single day will become positive contributions to your overall reformation.

Take note: Do not pursue health and fitness simply for vanity, do it so you will feel better about yourself—the collateral effect is that you'll begin to look good to other people. It's your life—you're the one who must look at your reflection in the mirror everyday. Do it for you. The secondary effects of other people noticing your nice figure are gratifying, but should not become your primary motivation.

grooming and personal hygiene

Starting from the very top of your head to the toes on your feet, here are tips on how to keep yourself looking your best.

HAIR

Having attractive, touchable hair is essential. Invest in a good stylist. Avoid going to those inexpensive, "no appointment needed" franchise beauty salons. If you wouldn't take your body to a bad doctor, don't take your hair to a bad hairdresser.

Ask your stylist what style or cut they think would look best on you. Look through magazines, tear out a page if you see something you like, and show it to them. Take your time; question them as to whether they think it would work with your bone structure and the texture of your hair. If you see someone on the street and you like the way their hair is cut, ask them where they got it done.

Women:

- **Teased hair:** High hair is out. If you tease your hair up, spritz so much hairspray that your head could be flammable, or look as if you've just returned from seeing a 1988 Bon Jovi concert, you are most definitely out of style.

- **Perms and curls:** Perms are out. If you weren't born with Mariah Carey's natural curls, it's probably best not to try and achieve the same look. You may wind up looking less like Mariah, and more like Little Orphan Annie. If you were granted curls instead of stick-straight strands, you'll have great hair as long as you take care of the side effects— by this I mean frizz. Invest in a good anti-frizz potion to tame the results of a humid day.

- **Short hair:** Short hair can be sexy, but only if you have the right-shaped face to carry it off. Before you chop off 10 inches of your locks, ask the person holding the scissors if they think short hair would work for you. If not, you may waste a lot of tears and time waiting for it to grow back.

- **Style:** Like acid wash and tie-dye, some styles can become seriously dated. High bangs and feathered wings are prime hair examples. Make sure to keep your hair up with the times. Check out some current magazines such as *Cosmopolitan, Marie Claire,* and *Elle,* or if you're older, look at a magazine that's more appropriate to your demographic. When you go to the stylist, while you're in the waiting area, look through the books of hairstyles sitting there. Make sure that your next trip to your stylist is not a trip back in time.

Men:
- **Mullets:** If you have anything that even resembles a mullet on the back of your head, cut it immediately. No one can pull off a mullet, not even Kid Rock. There's a reason why people have created entire Websites dedicated to poking fun at the mullet. I'll leave it at that.

- **Ponytails:** Steven Seagal cut his, and if you have one, it's time you followed suit. There are very few men in this world that can pull off long hair pulled into a ponytail, and chances are, they're up on the big screen wearing one for a role. Clean cut is in style. When was the last time you heard a woman remark, "Ponytails on men turn me on!"

- **Sideburns:** Sideburns can be extremely stylish if executed properly. However, if you wear them, make sure they're kempt. Bushy Elvis pork chops that cover your entire cheek should be left in the 70s with his rhinestone jumpsuits. Manicure them at least once a week, and you're in business.

• **Hair salons vs. Barbers:** Men should not be afraid of going to a good hairstylist. Barbers are okay, but they usually only cut one style reminiscent of your grandfather. Take some advice from a friend of the opposite sex and have them recommend a good salon for you. I guarantee you'll see as many men waiting to get shampooed as women.

• **Hair gel:** If you're going to use hair gel, don't overdo it. Women like hair that's soft and moveable, not hair they'll get a splinter from touching. If you have helmet head, it kills the fantasy.

• **Grease:** Wash your hair at least every two days. Grease isn't attractive unless you're Danny Zuko.

• **Balding:** If you're going bald, either become proud of it or do something to fix it. It's the people who can't make up their mind that end up a cocktail-party joke. Dermatologists can do amazing things with hair loss these days, from surgical re-placement to medication. If you don't mind balding, try having a stylist work with what you've got left. Usually, they'll cut it short all over. No matter what you think, leaving it long on the sides when you're balding on top is a grooming no-no. You'll look like Bozo the Clown. Women aren't at-tracted to clowns. If you're going bald, check out what others in fashion and in the entertainment business are doing to compensate for their shiny heads. Many times, you'll see that with the right glasses and your hair neatly cropped, you'll define a whole new sexy look. Never perform a comb-over unless you want to look like your high school principal and be laughed at behind your back.

- **Shaved heads:** Unless you're African American, I advise staying away from the shaved-head look. Many men who are not bald feel it necessary to shave their head to look like a cue ball. Why? Isn't it bad enough we have to deal with hair loss to begin with? Why are you trying to look old before your time? Some people think this is a good style, I don't. But I'll leave this one up to you.

EARS

Did you put a Q-tip in your ear this morning and pull out a candle? Don't let earwax get in the way of someone finding you attractive. It's easy to clean up and only takes ten seconds.

When you get out of the shower, take a Q-tip, and lightly rub around the inside of your ear. Don't push it into the ear; you'll hurt your eardrum. Just clean up the exterior and leave the interior for a doctor to cleanse. If you don't have time for a doctor, ask your local pharmacist about the best earwax-removal systems.

Women:
- **Earrings:** How many holes do you need? It's one thing to have a lot of piercings when you're young and in college, it's another thing when you're an adult and in the working world. No one wants to look at all that hardware. Keep your piercing to a minimum. A hole or two in each ear says confidence, sophistication, and class. Ten holes says you spend entirely too much time at the mall.

Men:

- **Earrings:** The late 80s and early 90s are gone. I know you're sad. It means you're growing older. But if you're still wearing earrings and you're not a rock star, you're out of style by at least ten years. Take out the metal, and let those babies close up. If male earrings come back in style, you can easily stick a pin back into your lobes and open them up again.

- **Ear hair:** Do you have blonde fuzz or dark hair growing from the rims of your ears or even from the inner canal? If so, get rid of it—no woman wants to look at your hairy ears! And when you start making out with a woman, she certainly doesn't want to lick and kiss them. Ears are very sensitive and erogenous, so you want them to be appealing and inviting. If you take care of them, it will pay back in spades of pleasure. Here are three alternatives for men with hairy ears. The most immediate is to buy a hair trimmer. (Don't shave them.) You can also have them waxed, although with this option, like using a hair trimmer, you'll have to repeat the process often. The best way is to get laser treatment. After three or four sessions, you'll never have to worry about fuzzy ears again.

EYES

The right glasses on both men and women can be very sexy, but coke bottle glasses aren't. Glasses are not just for reading or seeing. In today's world, they're also a fashion statement. They're displayed prominently on your face and should be selected carefully. If you think you're ready for a new pair, go to the nearest eyeglass store and bring a friend of the opposite sex whose sense of style you trust. Never be ashamed to get advice from a friend.

Some of you who wear glasses may also wear contact lenses. Contacts are a great investment and allow your full face to show. However, I strongly discourage you from getting colored contacts. It's false advertising. Imagine how disappointed someone will be who fell in love with your blue eyes, only to find out that they're actually brown. It wouldn't be earth shattering, but still, it's better to work with what you have. Besides, people fall in love with what is behind your eyes more than your actual eye color.

FACE

Both sexes need to care for their face. You only have one face, and as the years go by, any lack of care will begin to show. If you sit in the sun too much, you will prematurely wrinkle and also risk getting skin cancer. If you're often in the sun, be sure to wear a sunblock to protect yourself.

A common problem among both sexes is acne and for some, this problem goes beyond the teenage years. There are several medications on the market today, both prescription and over the counter, that can help clear up your complexion. Make an appointment with your dermatologist if you're suffering from acne blemishes.

Also, carefully examine whether or not you have whiteheads and/or blackheads on your face. There are many great day spas and places throughout the country to get facials. Men shouldn't be averse to getting a facial—it keeps your skin healthy and clean. When you go to get a facial, ask them to recommend facial lotions and cleansing creams. Put your face on a daily cleansing regimen. It will make you look younger and more vibrant

Women:

- **Makeup:** Makeup should always be used sparingly. If you spend an hour putting on makeup in the morning, you're spending fifty minutes too long. There's nothing attractive about someone who looks like they're wearing a mask. Lay off the heavy eyeliner and gothic black lipstick. Most men don't find it attractive.

    Some women wear makeup to cover up skin blemishes, which is fine, but be sure to learn the proper techniques to avoid streaking or blending problems. Many department stores offer expert advice on how to properly apply concealing products.

- **Facial hair:** Facial hair on women is not attractive. That goes for hair above the lip and the darker patches of hair that come down, near the ears, and look like sideburns. Waxing or laser treatments can take care of this problem.

Men:

- **Facial hair:** Here's a simple principle: If you aren't going to go clean shaven, then stick to a three-day growth at maximum. Up to a three-day growth is hot and sexy to women. Everything else has to go. That includes beards, goatees, bunny tails under the bottom lip, and mustaches. There are only a few men who can pull off full-blown facial hair. Guys like Steven Spielberg and Brad Pitt are among them. Of course, they're celebrities so anything they do is acceptable.

You, however, are not, so you must play by the normal rules of attraction.

Eyebrows

I once went out with a woman who shaved her eyebrows off and penciled them in. Despite her beauty, I couldn't help but wonder what she must look like after she took a shower, and the pencil had gone down the drain. Women, if you've shaved off your eyebrows, grow them back. If you're considering shaving them, don't. Most women have nice eyebrows and should simply get them waxed occasionally if necessary.

Men should manicure their eyebrows as well. There's nothing attractive about a uni-brow—you know, two eyebrows connected by a patch of hair right above your nose. If you have a uni-brow, get it waxed. If your problem isn't a uni-brow, but really bushy brows, get them trimmed. Bushy eyebrows detract from other facial features. When you go to a hairstylist, ask them for a brow snip.

Teeth

Your smile is one of the first things people notice about you. Many of us had braces to fix our teeth when we were young; some of us couldn't afford it. If you didn't have your teeth fixed when you were young and can afford it now, it's a worthwhile investment. There's no shame in wearing braces as an adult. In fact, these days, you don't even have to deal with those shiny railroad tracks. They now have invisible braces available. Call your dentist and look into it.

Next, check to see if your teeth are stained. Brown and yellow stains detract from your appearance. Many people who drink coffee, tea, or smoke cigarettes have this problem. These days, the solution is simple. You can either get your teeth whitened by laser or you can ask your dentist for a teeth-whitening formula. You'll have pearly whites in no time. If you don't have time to make an appointment with the dentist, check out your local pharmacy. Almost all of the major toothpaste companies have whiteners that you can easily purchase. After a few weeks, your teeth will be looking as white as they did before you discovered coffee.

On a related issue, many people have bad breath. It costs fifty cents to invest in some mints or a breath freshening spray. Many of us meet people after working hours—meaning after we've spent an entire day eating, drinking, or smoking. Don't approach someone when your breath stinks. It'll repel them from the get-go. Allow yourself a fighting chance by freshening up first.

LIPS

You can always enhance the appearance of your lips by making sure they're inviting. This means that they should never look chapped. It cost two dollars to buy a lip balm. When you go to the store to buy mints, invest in lip balm as well.

NOSE

Women and men both need to be careful of nose hair. If you have nose hair, clip it at least once a week. Nose hair clippers are fairly inexpensive.

Always check your nostrils in the bathroom mirror, and always carry a pack of tissues with you. They're cheap and disposable. You'd hate to meet the person of your dreams and have something dangling by a nose hair right in front of them. If you have to sneeze, sneeze into a tissue. Don't sneeze into your hand and then attempt to shake someone else's hand. Most of you know this already, however, you'd be surprised how many others don't.

NECK

The neck is a sensuous area that people kiss. Like your ears, people fantasize about kissing it. Take care of it. Here are some tips:

Women:
- **Jewelry:** It's always appropriate to wear necklaces. It's perfectly feminine and the right necklace will draw attention to your neck and upper torso.

Men:
- **Jewelry:** Men can wear a necklace as well, but keep it simple. Gaudy jewelry is a real turn-off to women. Wear a simple silver, gold, or white gold chain.

- **Razor bumps and Ingrown hairs:** Men frequently suffer from razor bumps and ingrown hairs in the neck area. Although there are shaving creams and special razors you can buy, I highly suggest calling your dermatologist. He or she can get to the root of the problem—no pun intended. Don't walk around with a puffy, rough looking neck.

CHEST

Some women love men with chest hair. With that said, I do subscribe to grooming common sense. Therefore, if you have a hairy chest, you need to trim. Men should never walk around with giant gobs of hair coming out of the top of their shirts. It's unnecessary. You can use a beard trimmer on your chest.

BACK

Chest hair may be sexy, but back hair never is. I know that some men like the way it feels when the wind blows through their back hair on a warm summer day at the beach, but trust me, it doesn't compare to the feeling you get when a woman massages your hairless back. You can either have your back waxed or you can get the hair removed by laser. Waxing is painful, but worth it. The hair that grows back will decrease with every waxing. The alternative is laser removal, which can be very expensive. Of course, when your treatment is done, the hair will be gone forever.

ARMS

A few weeks ago I was at a convenience store when a very attractive woman walked in. Her face and style attracted me—until I saw her bare forearms, which were extremely hairy. If you're a woman with very dark arm hair, the easiest way to de-emphasize it is to bleach it. Men can also take care to keep their arm hair in check by trimming. No woman wants to see a guy roll up his sleeves, only to reveal the gorilla that hides under his shirt.

HANDS

Hands, like a smile, are observed quickly. Women especially notice nice hands on men. Why? Because they enjoy imagining those hands on their body and face. Here are a few tips for both sexes.

Women:
- **Fingernails:** I don't need to tell women to get manicures. Women generally love manicures. However, I recommend staying away from funky nail polish and art designs. Art design on your fingernails says you spend too much time in the nail salon. It's cheesy. Black fingernail polish relays that you're interested in death. Not something you want to express before a conversation even takes place. Keep it simple.

Men:
- **Fingernails:** Men, don't be afraid of getting your nails manicured. You're not a wimp if you do. As a matter of fact, when you have a beautiful new lady on your arm, you can laugh at all your macho friends who laughed at you for being a metrosexual. Women like men with hands and fingernails that are smooth and kempt. That means no dirt, no bleeding skin from biting, and nails that won't scratch them to death. If you bite your nails, go to the pharmacy and buy the special polish that deters you from biting away. It tastes really awful and after the first time you go to chew, you will be stopped from going back a second time.

- **Hairy knuckles:** Sometimes men have hairy knuckles. If you do, take a small pair of scissors or hair trimmer and clean them up.

- **Jewelry:** Again, watch out for gaudy jewelry. Men should never wear diamonds or gold nugget rings. Remember, gold is not as hip as it may once have been. If you want to wear a ring, do so, just not on the pinky. Pinky rings are for mobsters, not for you. Take note: Less is more.

FEET

Feet are like cats; you either love them or hate them. I happen to think feet are cute. Other people find them to be horrifying. As a general rule, both men and women should get pedicures. Not only will they clip your nails, but they will also remove the dead skin from your tootsies. Some establishments even give you a foot and leg massage after they're done. In the summertime, men should trim down the hairy toe knuckles. As with hairy hand knuckles, a small pair of scissors will do the trick.

style for men

Too many times in my life and career I've heard women complain about the way men dress. However, to a large extent, I'd have to agree with them. Most men, including my clients, never take the time to figure out what's in style and what styles complement their body type. Generally, women spend countless hours thumbing through fashion magazines and in stores trying on different clothing. As you will read in the next section, Style for Women, not all women make the right choices. However, they generally try harder than most men.

There's no shame in men spending time looking through magazines such as *GQ* and *Esquire* to find out what the hot new looks are. In addition, there's no shame is spending an entire day in a store trying on clothing. Contrary to some people's opinion, it doesn't make you vain or materialistic—it makes you smart.

Unless you are living on a hippie commune, everyday we present ourselves to a wide array of people in the world. Throughout the days and nights of our lives we present ourselves to our friends, family, coworkers, bosses, existing clients, potential new clients, and potential new love interests. And one of the first things that anyone will notice about you is your clothing and how you wear it. It's worth your time investment to find the right clothes so that you can help market yourself the right way. Whether we like it or not, we live in a time of marketing, and it's very difficult in our fast-paced world to get people to take a second look after a bad first impression.

There are many resources available for men to learn more about style. However, until you have read your share of books and magazines, pick someone who has taste you trust, and ask them to spend a day with you shopping. Sometimes it helps to bring someone of the opposite sex. If you do, make sure that they understand that you want them to be brutally honest with you about what looks good and what doesn't. In the meantime, I have included some tips that I give my clients within the first weeks of working with me.

Remember, you don't have to spend loads of money to look

good—you just have to be smart about where you shop and what you buy. You can look like a million bucks without spending a million bucks. And once you are in the right clothing and you are confident in how you look, you'll have a whole new positive attitude that will increase your chances of attracting a date.

SUITS

Almost every man must wear a suit at one time or another. While many must wear them to the office on a daily basis, there are others that only wear a suit on special occasions. In either case, all men should know where to buy a suit, how to buy a suit, how the suit should fit, and how to accessorize the suit for the greatest impact. Since books have been written on this subject and are available at any bookstore, I'm just going to touch upon a few of the basics.

Although throughout much of the country the trend for the workplace has become business casual, many men are confronted with the requirement of a whole new, more formal wardrobe for themselves. With five days to a workweek, many men are faced with a daunting and expensive challenge—to build a sharp business wardrobe on a limited budget.

Suits not only represent you in the business world, they will also help put your best foot forward at after-work social functions where you may interact with members of the opposite sex. You'll want to buy the best suits you can afford. If it helps ease the pain of spending the money, think of buying good suits as an investment in your financial and social future.

However, the bill shouldn't kill you either. Taking into account the suits and the accessories you'll need (such as shirts, ties, shoes, socks, belts, and cuff links), it is relatively easy to ensure that your total clothing bill doesn't come out to more than $3,500. For those of you on a tighter budget, there are many great discount chain stores that sell basic suits at lower prices. Since you'll be rotating these five suits on a weekly basis, it's best to stick with dark, conservative colors with simple patterns that you can easily match with different shirts and ties for variety. A complicated pattern on your suit will be easily recognizable to your coworkers as a suit you've worn over and over again.

The following is my advice for a starter series:

- Men in the business world should buy a solid-blue suit, a subtly patterned blue suit, a subtly patterned brown suit, a gray pinstripe, and either a black or blue pinstripe. This will give you some freedom to mix it up and, as I said, allow you to add a lot of different ties and shirts, which is much less costly than buying new suits.

- If you're not in the business world, you should at least have a blue or black suit that you can wear on special occasions.

- Two- and three-button suits are in style and depending on your body type, a double-breasted jacket can be extremely fashionable.

- The suit should fit you well and should not be baggy or too tight to button.

- Your pants can either be pleated or flat front. Although flat front is considered the latest rage, it's really a matter of preference since they're both perfectly acceptable. If you purchase flat-front pants, there should be no cuff on the pants. However, if you buy pleats, a cuff is always recommended.

- Your suit sleeve length should always allow a little bit of the cuff of your shirt to show.

- Find a good tailor to help you with all the minor adjustments. If you see a friend who has particularly well-fitting suits, ask him which tailor worked on his clothes.

In addition to having nice suits, it's important to wear the right accessories. Accessories will give you the variety you need and will make getting dressed for workweek after workweek more fun and less cumbersome. Remember, your five basic suits are just a starter series. Once you have these staples in your wardrobe, you can begin to build upon them with different patterns and colors.

For now, you should only stock up on the basics. For instance, with the five basic suits I mentioned, you'll only need two pairs of nice dress shoes, in black and brown, with dress belts to match. I recommend square-tipped shoes as a start. They're young and sharp looking, and can also be worn with a pair of slacks. Stock up on dress socks in brown, gray, black, and blue that won't fall down around your ankles. Additionally, you should buy at least three basic white shirts and three blue shirts with straight collars, that don't have buttons. For a more refined look, you can buy at least one shirt in each color with French cuffs and get some silver cuff links in either a plain or funky design—you can get a little creative here, but again, stay away from anything too flashy. It's the little things that make a difference.

Finally, invest in some nice, conservative ties. Get an array of colors with simple patterns. You should avoid ties that are either too shiny or too dull. There are thousands upon thousands of ties out there for you to choose in stripes, plaids, and paisley. Pick what fits your personality, but try to keep things simple. The right tie will take the emphasis off the suit you wore four times that month.

The wonderful thing about owning suits is that you don't just have to wear them for work or fancy occasions. You can dress suits down by wearing an open collar or throwing on a sport shirt underneath—perhaps a turtleneck in the winter, or a polo shirt in the summer. Also, you can wear the pants from each suit without the jacket, and the jackets with a pair of jeans. With a starter wardrobe of five suits and accessories, you have the capacity to put together countless outfits.

JEANS

The right jeans will draw attention from members of the opposite sex. However, styles do come and go with jeans, so it's important to stay on top of what's hot and what's not.

For those of you out there who are still wearing acid-wash or two-tone jeans, immediately grab a garbage bag and toss them. Acid-wash jeans were awful when they first came out and are even worse today. People, let it go.

Take a member of the opposite sex with you to purchase your jeans. Don't just choose anyone. Pick someone with a great sense of style. This probably doesn't mean your mother and your most likely better off with your sister. If you can't find anyone to go with you, go to a cool, hip, boutique-type store, and ask the salesgirl what she would recommend. Then, try them on and ask her for her honest opinion. Most of the time, she'll give it to you.

When you visit a store to try on jeans, try on every style you can get your hands on. Spend an entire day trying on different styles and sizes. You won't know what looks good on you until you have a frame of reference. Don't just go out and buy a pair of jeans you saw on your friend. The jeans he bought could look totally different on you. Take your time. If you consider the amount of time you spend wearing jeans, it's worth being extra cautious to find the right ones.

If the jeans feel too tight or too baggy, then chances are they don't fit you. I hate walking down the street and seeing men's underwear sticking out of the back of their overly baggy jeans. Who decided that was cool? It's the worst thing to come out of the hip-hop generation since Vanilla Ice.

One of the wonderful things about jeans that we all love is that jeans show off our figures. If you've got a good butt, pull up those pants and show it off. Ask any woman what she thinks of Lenny Kravitz's butt and then ask her if she'd prefer him to wear baggy pants. If you don't have a great butt, just find something that fits right. Not everyone can be Lenny, but the right pair of jeans can de-emphasize your shortcomings. Just keep in mind that if they look more like spandex than denim, they're probably a little too tight.

Lastly, if you're vertically challenged, get your jeans hemmed. If your jeans are too long, they'll bunch up at the bottom and you'll look like a slob. Conversely, if you're tall and the bottoms of the jeans are too short, you'll look like you got caught in a flood. Tell the tailor that you want a small break at the bottom. In addition, when you do get your jeans fixed, tell the tailor you want the original seam put back, or your jeans won't lay the right way and won't look right. Another tip when looking at jeans is to make sure that you've got two great pairs of jeans that you can wear out on the weekend. It's okay if you spend a little more than you think you should—a great pair of jeans always pays off in the end.

PANTS

Like jeans, you should take your time finding great-fitting pants. Make sure they fit correctly in the crotch and in the rear, and that they don't flare at the sides or hug your body too tightly. Have them hemmed as you would your jeans or your suit pants—with a small break at the bottom.

If you're going to buy simple pants to wear casually, I recommend flat-fronts. Unlike suit pants, there's no jacket to cover up the front of your pants. Therefore, it's important to have a clean, sharp look. Flat-front pants have that look both from the front and from the side, and can be paired with a simple belt.

As staples in your wardrobe, you should invest in at least three pairs of pants in colors such as gray, black, and brown. Take note: Dark conservative colors are universally versatile and flattering. If you're overweight, you should know that dark colors are slenderizing and will give you a slimmer appearance. With that said, overweight people should try to avoid wearing light colored pants such as khakis. As a matter of fact, I feel that khakis look good on few people and should only be worn by those who are certain they can pull off that look. There are far better choices out there these days—you don't always have to go for the Dockers.

SHIRTS

There are a million different types of shirts. There are dress shirts, casual button downs, sweatshirts, T-shirts, pullovers, pullovers with collars, sweaters, long-sleeved shirts, short-sleeved shirts, and polo shirts. The list goes on and on. I simply can't address all of the different types of shirts available to you and I wouldn't even try. However, I will give you a few general thoughts.

Shirts are like billboards. When you see someone walking down the street, their shirt is the first thing you see. Usually, our chests are the widest part of our body, and for that reason, it's important to carefully choose what we put on. Here are a few basic shirt rules: First, dark colors are slenderizing, while light colors are not. If you're thin, you should mix up your wardrobe with lighter colors. If you're overweight, you should invest in darker colors. Second, vertical stripes will make you look thinner, while horizontal stripes will accentuate heaviness around the midsection. Always invest in shirts that are made of high-quality material, and make sure you take care of them according to their labeling. You should never machine wash a shirt that calls for dry cleaning, or you may ruin it. Avoid buying rough, itchy material, or even material that looks like it may fade easily.

You should invest in basic button downs in basic colors such as black, brown, gray, and blue. You can wear them with jeans, slacks, or even under a sweater. Remember, if you're going to buy patterned shirts, make sure they're up to date patterns. For example stay away from Hawaiian shirts if you're not in Hawaii. Finally, if the design of the shirt allows, you may consider wearing it without tucking it in.

T-SHIRTS

One type of shirt that I believe deserves its own section is the T-shirt. I love T-shirts. T-shirt designers have become as hot as the biggest fashion designers. These days, some T-shirts sell for over $200. The quality of a T-shirt is something that you need to look into. Try to find a shirt that fits you and really defines your body. I hate seeing men wearing T-shirts that drape downward without any shape. There are many brands on the market and I suggest that you go to the mall and find the brands that are the most flattering to you. It's worth spending the extra money— remember that you're marketing yourself to the opposite sex and part of that marketing is to work on the package that you present. You don't want to look like someone who's wearing a shirt that doesn't fit—it's unflattering.

SHOES

Women love shoes and they also love men who wear nice shoes. They especially like a man who wears nice shoes and takes good care of them. From sneakers to boots there are many different types of shoes that range from formal to casual.

First, always buy sharp black and brown shoes to go with your suits. Second, buy black and brown shoes to go with your jeans or pants. Different shoes go with different pants. Third, get some cool boots. Not to worry, I don't mean cowboy boots. Every guy should have a pair of boots to go with a pair of jeans. It's a great look and makes short men appear taller.

Always make sure you own a pair or two of sneakers that

you wouldn't wear to the gym. You should never wear gym shoes with jeans. It's an awful and sloppy look. There are many fun and retro sneakers that are not meant for the gym, and look great with jeans. Be conscientious of what you choose—make sure to get a pair of sneakers that will be versatile enough for you to wear with a combination of outfits.

ACCESSORIES

I briefly touched on accessories, but I'll reiterate a few points. First, if you're going to wear jewelry, make it silver or white gold and keep it simple. I would never recommend wearing a ring, a bracelet, and a necklace at the same time. It's overkill. When in doubt, go with the old adage, "Keep it simple, stupid." Second, invest in nice belts. Belts, like shoes, are different for formal and casual occasions. Buy simple at first, and then build on your collection. Never wear the dress belts you wear with your suits, with your jeans. Instead, invest in casual belts in addition to your dress belts. Third, get nice socks. Socks, too, are divided into formal and casual categories. Never wear white socks with dress shoes and never *ever* wear socks with sandals. Obviously, you should never wear gym socks with a suit, and rarely should you wear dress socks with jeans. Fourth, get a killer watch. Watches can catch people's eye, and will help draw attention to you. It's worth the investment. You may even want to get two—one for suits, and one for casual occasions. Finally, if possible, you should try to invest in a leather coat. While black and brown are always safe bets, if you can only get one, make sure to choose the color that goes with the most clothing in your closet.

style for women •••

A large part of my work with my female clients involves taking them shopping in order to find them a look that will make them feel better about themselves and in turn make them more appealing to the opposite sex. As a dating coach and image maker, my job is to know what gets a man's attention. For my female clients, my goal is simple—I help them market themselves to the kind of men they're looking to attract.

With that said, women, like men, come in all shapes and sizes. This means that women need to try to look at themselves objectively in order to find looks that are flattering to their particular body type. Unfortunately, one of the biggest mistakes a woman can make is buying clothing that is neither weight nor age appropriate. Men are visual creatures and know more about women's fashion than you may think they do.

As a first step, you should try to appeal to a man's visual senses by marketing yourself appropriately. To accomplish this, you must keep in mind the type of man that you're trying to attract. If you're looking for a younger man, you'll need to come up with a more youthful look for yourself. If you want to attract a conservative man, you will need to dress that part. Keep in mind that you should feel comfortable in the look that you choose. If you know that you'd feel awkward going out for an evening in a short skirt and a fitted sleeveless shirt, I don't recommend forcing yourself into the look. It will be obvious to anyone who sees or approaches you that you're uncomfortable in your own skin. The more confidence you present in your packaging, the more likely you are to attract the type of guy you went out looking for.

There are many ways to find the kind of look you want before even hitting the stores. My best advice is to browse through magazines and catalogues to find women who are built similar to you, and see what looks flattering on those particular models. For example, if you're overweight, look at plus-size models. If you're petite, pay careful attention to shorter women or the petite lines of clothing that so many catalogue clothing companies are now offering. By doing so, you will have a good idea of what you're looking to buy when venturing out to stores. Or if you don't want to venture outdoors, you may shop online. When shopping at an online retailer, the outfits are often already put together on the models—you can either look for a similar ensemble in the stores, or order that very outfit if you think it would look good on you. Many online stores have great return policies if what you've bought doesn't fit right or isn't what you really wanted.

Another great way to achieve your desired look is to pay attention to what other women around you are wearing. If you like what you see, ask them where they bought their clothes—I find that women love to talk about the great sales they found, or where they like to go shopping. Try to shop at stores where the salespeople aren't just trying to make a commission, and really want to help you find something flattering. I've been in far too many stores where a salesperson will be asked for an opinion and will let someone buy something all wrong just to make a sale. If you sense that this is the case, you can always get a second opinion from a fellow shopper or another salesperson. Never feel pressured to buy something your intuition is telling you not to buy. It's also a good idea to develop a relationship with the people at your local boutiques and favorite mall stores. When they get clothes in stock that they think would be good for you, you can ask them to give you a call. It's a great way to ensure that they'll always have your size.

SUITS

In today's business world many women are required to wear suits just as often as men are. The right suit on a woman can be a show of strength, power, and confidence, and at the same time convey a tremendous amount of sex appeal. Like a man's suit, a woman's suit should be complementary to their form.

While the trend in the American business world has moved toward a business-casual dress code, women are often faced with the challenge of having to acquire a whole new wardrobe when starting a new job. Although this may seem like an overwhelming task, it's relatively easy for women to build a great look for themselves on a limited budget. Keep in mind, not only does a great business ensemble keep you looking your best at work, but it'll also go far toward helping you look great for any after-work events.

If you're required to wear suits, I recommend basic colors. You should purchase staple colors such as black, navy, gray, and brown. These colors are classic and will give you a solid base on which to build. If solids are too plain for your taste, you can also experiment with a simple pinstripe pattern. Always keep the quality of the material in mind. A better quality material will always make a suit look better. Remember that the more basic the suit, the more you will be able to mix and match.

Jackets can either be a classic single-breasted or double-breasted. The length of the jacket should fall to around the palm of your hand if you were standing with hands by your sides. The shoulders shouldn't be too boxy or sloped and definitely shouldn't have heavy padding. Shoulder pads should be left back in the 80s—there's no reason for a woman in a suit to look like a line-backer. A great-looking suit jacket can also double as a blazer over a pair of jeans, and can be worn for a night out, or on casual Fridays if your company allows it.

As opposed to men, women have the option of wearing either a pair of pants or a skirt with their suit. Both are perfectly acceptable in the business world. For variety, you may want to buy both the skirt and the pair of pants that match the jacket. If wearing a skirt, you should stick with hosiery while in the workplace.

If you choose pants, you must select flat-fronts. Flat-fronts are slenderizing. A good pair of flat-front suit pants can also be paired with a dressy top for an evening out on the town, or a special occasion. Cuffed pant legs are more formal, while uncuffed pants elongate the leg. You should choose the style that is flattering to your body type and comfortable. If you have to wear it all day long at the office, there's no reason to be uncomfortable and spend your day wishing you could slip on a pair of sweatpants.

Women should also keep in mind that they'll need to purchase accessories to wear their suits, which is why it's best to keep the suits simple. Accessories are where one can really get creative. Blouses, shoes, and jewelry in an array of colors and styles can add flair and variety to your suits, and help to detract from the fact that you'll need to rotate your outfits for awhile. The shirt under a suit can be anything from a refined button down to a thin, fitted sweater. If you buy these items in an assortment of colors, patterns, and fabrics, then you can easily match them with more than one of your suits, as well as other bottoms such as a skirt, a pair of pants or jeans. When choosing shoes for a suit, it's best to stick with basic colors and styles. Again, a nice pair of shoes worn with a suit may also be worn with a nice pair of pants or a skirt and top. The more you accessorize, the more wear you'll get from your wardrobe. Accessories are also far less of an expensive purchase than a whole new suit. If you choose your accessories carefully, you can put together many fashionable looks with one basic suit and have more than enough clothing to get you through a month without repeating the same outfit.

JEANS

Unlike men, women usually wear their jeans tight. Therefore, jeans are perhaps the most revealing piece of clothing a woman can put on. They hug the female form and as a result can draw a lot of attention to the person wearing them! Unfortunately, many women try to wear jeans that are not appropriate to their body style. If you know you're on the overweight side, I recommend not buying low waisted, hip hugger–type jeans. You should look for styles that sit a bit higher on the waist, and perhaps have an easier, looser fit. It's never attractive to see a woman walking down the street with her stomach and sides hanging over the edge of her denim. In contrast, if your body type allows it, you should look for jeans that are hip-slung and fitted that will complement your shape.

Women must constantly keep on top of the jeans trend. As I told men in the previous section, if you're a woman and still wearing two tone or acid wash, burn them. They're out of style. What's on the market now is far superior to what was on the market just a few years ago. Now, jeans are made for all body types, in all sizes, in all cuts, and in all washes and colors. All women should invest in at least two pairs of great jeans. Be warned—great jeans can be costly. Jeans for women have become the new evening wear. These days, it's more than acceptable for women to wear a nice pair of jeans to go out on the town. As a result, a great pair of jeans is a great investment and should be chosen carefully. After all, you'll probably wear them far more than any other article of clothing.

When you buy jeans, try on every style you can find, in every fade and wash. Make sure you're shopping at a great store and ask a salesperson, whose style you like, to help you find the right pair of denim. Ask them how the fit looks in the leg, at the waist, and especially in the butt. You don't want jeans that crawl up the butt or, alternatively, look baggy in the rear. Take your time to find the right pair that makes you look and feel good. Keep in mind that above all, jeans should complement your figure. Therefore, no matter how bad you want that new pair of Diesels that your friend Karen just got, make sure before you buy them, that they look just as good on you as they do on her.

If you're a taller woman, make sure that the jeans you buy are long enough in the leg. Jeans that are too short never look good on anyone. If you're a shorter woman, make sure to hem your jeans if they're too long. All women should always take their shoes into account when altering the length of their jeans.

Women wear different shoes with different jeans, and these shoes can vary in the height of the heel. If you know you're going to wear a pair of your jeans with a pair of boots that have a higher heel, make sure that you bring the boots with you to a tailor so that they may take this account when figuring out the amount to remove from the bottom. Also, when having your jeans hemmed, make sure the tailor replaces the original hem. This will make the alterations less noticeable, and help the jeans lay correctly at the bottom.

PANTS

Unlike men, women have the option of buying either loose- or form-fitting pants. Women should own at least three pairs of slacks in colors such as black, gray, brown, and navy. Slacks come in a variety of styles and cuts, from low waisted to higher waisted. You should be careful to choose the style that looks best on you. Keep in mind that the pant leg openings should never be too narrow or tapered. Make sure that the material of the pants is a quality fabric, or they may not last more than a few trips to the laundry or cleaners. A great pair of pants can be coupled with a variety of tops, giving you more in your closet to choose from.

SKIRTS

As men we love to look at women in skirts. A great skirt can either be long or short, depending on the occasion. If you have terrific legs, you should have no problem wearing a short skirt. However, if you know that your legs are on the thicker side, you should stick with longer skirts that fall below the knee. Sometimes, less can be more. A skirt doesn't have to come right below your bottom to be sexy. Pick a skirt for yourself that you feel good in, in a pattern or fabric that can be paired with many different tops. Skirts come in many styles and cuts, from pleated to A-line. Jean skirts are a great staple for any wardrobe. They can be dressed up for a night out, or dressed down for a day at the beach, and come in as many styles, lengths and washes as a regular pair of jeans. Just remember your desired look, who you're trying to attract, and to feel good in what you have on.

TOPS

When shopping for any great top, you need to think about what you're going to wear it with. Shirts for women come in an endless variety of styles, patterns, fabrics, and colors, many of which can actually double for work and play. Again, a look at the current magazines will give you an idea of what's in style at the moment. After all, tie die was the "in" look years ago, but wouldn't be considered a fashionable look today.

When buying tops, you should try to look for things that can be worn with more than one type of bottom. For example, there are many great fitted button-down shirts that can be worn under a suit or on top of a pair of jeans. When shopping, you can ask the sales person if they think that the shirt you've chosen would look good with a pair of jeans, a skirt, and a pair of dress pants. Again, never be afraid to ask.

T-Shirts

A great fitting T-shirt can really complement a woman's figure and will help add some casual style to any wardrobe. T-shirts are far more important than many tend to think. There are many men out there who love the look of a woman in a great T-shirt and a pair of jeans. Always keep in mind when picking out your T-shirts that there are many different styles, cuts, and fabrics, and not all may be right for you. Experiment by trying on T-shirts that are plain cotton, ribbed, have a pattern or design, have some stretch, a scoop neck, a crewneck, and a v-neck to see which one fits your body type the best. Try to avoid anything baggy and oversized. If you're on the overweight side, you can still find something that's flattering without buying it three sizes too big.

Women should also keep in mind that a T-shirt can either play up or play down the size of their chests. If you're a woman who is well-endowed and prefers not to call attention to it, you may want to invest in T-shirts that are fitted, but not skin tight, that have a higher neckline. You may also want to avoid T-shirts with sayings or words across the chest area. In contrast, if you're looking to make the most of what you were given, you may want to look into T-shirts that are on the tighter side. The point here is to do a little research and try on many brands and styles until you find the one that fits right.

Shoes

Never wear gym sneakers with jeans—gym sneakers should be left in your locker where they belong. Instead, invest in some great modern retro sneakers that can be worn instead of the shoes you just ran two miles in. They are just as comfortable to walk around in as your running shoes, but have a lot more style. When looking at shoes, you'll also need to distinguish the difference between dress shoes to be worn with work clothes and casual shoes to be worn for a fun date—you should have at least two good pairs of shoes suitable for each occasion. Be sure to invest in a good pair of boots that go well with jeans, as well as a pair to go with dress pants and a skirt. Shoes can make or break an outfit, so be careful and take your time when picking out a pair.

ACCESSORIES

Most women I know love accessories, and have the capability to be far more creative in this department than men. If you want to dress up your wardrobe, you can always add hats, scarves, belts, and a cool bag. Just remember to keep it simple and to not overdo it. Always remember to be as creative as possible, and never forget your marketing tactics.

concluding the physical makeover

Congratulations. You've just finished the physical makeover section of this book. Now you should be ready to go out and take care of a few necessary changes and make some improvements. Go get that haircut, clean those ears, get yourself a manicure, and do a little shopping. Treat yourself. Remember, if you're to be successful in dating, you have to prepare yourself for the challenge. You now have the mind-set, grooming habits, and attire to go back into the dating world. In the next section, I will teach you the rest of the skills that you'll need for dating successfully. For now, take a look at the physical makeover checklist on the following page.

CHECKLIST

- Exercise.

- Get a haircut. Make sure it's in style. No mullets please.

- Get fashionable glasses or contacts, or both.

- Trim your eyebrows or wax them.

- Get a facial. Lighten up on the makeup.

- Get your teeth whitened.

- Buy lip balm.

- Buy pocket tissues to clean your nose. Carry them with you.

- Remove unnecessarily flashy jewelry. Remember, stick with silver, or white gold. Less is more.

- Remove unnecessary body hair: Beards, ears, back, chest, arms, hand knuckles, and toe knuckles. Women, shave those legs and bleach or wax where necessary.

- Get a manicure and pedicure.

- When shopping, keep the staples simple in order to maximize what's in your closet.

- Be mindful of who you're marketing yourself to.

- Never be afraid to ask a salesperson for their opinion.

- Take your time in finding what looks best on you.

- Get creative.

- Have fun!

when and where to meet people

Lonely people are everywhere. Still, the complaint that I hear most often from new clients is that they're unsuccessful in finding and making contact with new people to date. They lead full and busy professional lives. They participate in all kinds of extracurricular committees and belong to different types of clubs. They eat out, go to the movies, and exercise at the gym. They might even stake out the most popular nightspots every Friday and Saturday. Still, they can't find anyone to date.

So, why do my clients have such a problem? Generally, it's because they're not really looking—or shall I say, trying. Many times they simply have the wrong outlook and often don't make themselves available. Most of the time, however, they're simply not taking advantage of all of the available resources to meet other "lonely" people.

In the 21st century, single people can be found just about everywhere. These days, you don't even have to leave the house to meet a bevy of new companions—you can sit in your pajamas eating Crunch and Munch at three in the morning and meet people simply by logging into cyberspace. So, if you're one of those people who complains to your friends that there's a lack of available prospects—stop right now! That excuse no longer works.

You just may have to face the fact that you haven't been going about it the right way. Whenever you start thinking that there isn't anyone to date, I want you to reflect on the fact that there are over 82 million singles in the United States today alone. All readers take note—there are never a lack of prospects or opportunities to meet people to date, only a lack of willingness to be proactive. Even if you live in a small town in Iowa.

In this section of the book, I'm going to discuss the three main ways that you can go about getting dates. First, there are blind dates where you are set up by someone with someone you don't know or don't know well. Second, through cyberspace. Meeting people on the Internet is quasi-blind dating. It's true that you don't know the person you're meeting, but instead of someone else making the introduction, you're doing it yourself using a portal as the introducing party. Third, by meeting people while going about your daily activities, or as I like to say meeting people about town. Meeting people about town is the good old-fashioned way of meeting people, and later we will explore almost every place you can find people while you're out and about.

Each of the aforementioned ways to meet new people to date are distinct in that they require a different set of skills in the initial stages. For instance, to be set up on a blind date, one only needs to make a phone call or pick up the phone. The hard work of the introduction is already done for you. With the Internet, you must do the hard work yourself and make contact with a person in such a way that will ensure either you or they will pick up the phone to make the next move. However, meeting people around town is by far the most complicated, and requires its own skill set. This approach is what causes the most anxiety to people and is the most shrouded in mystery—but can also be extremely effective. For that reason, Step 3 of this book, Making Contact, will be dedicated to the interpersonal communication skills you need to master for meeting people about town.

All three ways to meet new people are fun and should be done in conjunction with one another to maximize your chances of finding one person you really like. Remember, lonely people are everywhere. By not using one of the three ways to meet people, you are eliminating a steady stream of potential love interests. You should maximize your chances, not eliminate them. You never know where "The One" will come from. Of course, you won't like everyone you go out with. You have to try on a lot of different hats to find one that fits. Trying on those hats is part of the journey we discussed in Step 1. There will always be good and bad experiences—so it's the journey we must enjoy.

When you're done reading this part of the book, you'll see that I've covered most of the typical places where anyone would be able to meet someone. Of course, it would be impossible to think of every scenario. Therefore, you must be able to be creative as opportunity arises.

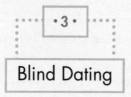

Blind Dating

It's Wednesday night. Dana has just come home after a long day. After work, she went to the gym, and then, on the way home, bought herself a salad for dinner. All she wants to do is change clothes, drop onto the sofa, eat, and tune into her favorite reality dating show. Just as she's beginning to unwind, the phone rings.

Dana rolls her eyes, unsure if she should answer it. Yet, of course, she can't resist. After all, what if it's her boss telling her she got a promotion? What if it's her friend, who just inherited half a million dollars, telling her she's taking her to Europe? What if it's her ex-boyfriend calling her to apologize for breaking her heart and he wants her back? Her head swimming, Dana eagerly grabs the phone.

"Hello?"

"Dana, it's your mother," the familiar voice hollers from the other end of the line—as if Dana wouldn't have recognized her own mother's voice after twenty-nine-years. Dana slumps back into the couch.

"Hi Mom," Dana says, despondent, her dreams of money, Europe, and reconciliation crushed beneath her mother's New York accent.

"Listen, have I got the perfect person for you. His name is Saul Burgerstein. He's your Aunt Martha's best friend's third cousin. He's living in Atlanta not far from you. He's supposed to be a great catch. An accountant."

Dana puts the television on mute. She's silent. She knows her mother's intentions are good, but she hates blind dates. From her experience, they never work out. In addition, Aunt Martha and Dana have completely different ideas of what a "good catch" is. After all, Martha married Dana's Uncle Henry. A nice man mind you, but Dana had seen pictures of her uncle in his twenties, and would have never gone out with him had she been Martha. However, Dana humors her mother.

"Is he good looking?" she asks.

"I have no idea," Dana's mother says. "He may be, he may not. What does it matter? Have a drink with the man. It can't hurt."

"I don't know," Dana replies, skeptical.

"You know what your problem is? You have a bad attitude," Dana's mother says, laying into her. "You're too picky. It's not like you're dating anyone right now, anyway. And Dana, I'm not getting any younger here. If you don't get married and have children soon, someday when you do, your kids won't have grandparents. We'll be dead."

Dana puts the phone down, upset from her mother's double blow. First, in regard to the fact that she isn't dating anyone and second, guilt about her grand-parentless children. Yet, Dana puts the phone back to her ear.

"Fine, mother. I'll go," Dana says.

"Thank God," Dana's mother responds. "I already said I'd talked to you and you agreed. He's calling you tomorrow."

"Goodnight, mother," Dana says as she hangs up the phone.

How many of you reading this have encountered a scenario similar to Dana's? Unless you were one of the lucky few that found a life partner in college or soon thereafter, you probably have. Yep, the majority of us have a mother, an Aunt Martha, and a Saul Burgerstein.

Blind dates with the Saul Burgersteins of the world can come to you from a variety of sources such as your family, your friends, or even coworkers. Our first reactions to these match-making attempts can be skewed by our own prior unsuccessful attempts at blind dating. However, no matter how jaded you are, from this point forward you must try to look at blind dating as an opportunity to meet new people to date. You never know when a Saul or even a Sally Burgerstein could be just the person you were looking for.

Remember, the goal of this book is not to find the love of your life on your first attempt. The goal is help you realize all of the available avenues to meet new people so that you expand your potential to meet the love of your life down the road. You never know where that love is going to come from and you should never turn your nose up at an opportunity to meet some-one new. Most people are strangers before they fall in love with each other—at least with blind dating you have an intermediary, someone in common who thinks highly of both of you.

Again, you may not find the love of your life on the first attempt or even the tenth. It could take a hundred. However, even if it took a hundred blind dates, wouldn't it be worth your time and effort if it meant finding the right person for you? Remember, you have to play the numbers and date as many people as you can to find someone you mesh with. Blind dating is just another arena for you to explore along your journey.

Everything is a journey and dating is no different. It's a process by which you learn about yourself and the people you share the world with. Although you may not like everyone you encounter in the world, you can take every dating experience you have with you throughout your life, and that may benefit you down the road when you finally do come in contact with someone you mesh with. Blind dating simply provides another way for you to evolve and improve your interpersonal communication skills.

Whenever you go on a date, any date, remember to observe, listen, and ask questions—even if it's someone you know you're not attracted to. If you can't take away love from the date, take away something. Better yourself. Everyone has something to offer and everyone's an expert at least at one thing. Find out who your date is and what makes them tick, rather than sitting there and trying to figure out ways to get home. After all is said and done, they may become an ally of yours—a friend, an expansion of your dating network, or even a business contact. Always look to expand your network of allies.

how to get a blind date ···

Usually, blind dating is initiated when someone you know wants to introduce you to someone they know. However, sometimes, it can be that you don't even know the introducing intermediary. Like the Saul Burgerstein scenario, my mother once called me and told me she had a friend who I'd never met, who had seen my picture and wanted to set me up with her niece who lived in New York.

Whether you know the intermediary or not, the scene usually plays out the same way. One person receives the contact information and that person is responsible for getting the ball rolling. These days, contact information comes in the form of either a phone number or an e-mail address.

WHEN YOU'RE THE CONTACTOR

The Contactor is the one responsible for contacting the other person and asking them on a date. If you're the Contactor, find out as much information as you can about the other person before you make the first phone call or write that first e-mail. Being prepared with such information will aid you in what many people find to be an awkward conversation. It will give you more to talk about other than the person you both have in common. Try to find out what their relationship to the intermediary is, where they went to school, where they live, what their hobbies are. Do not focus on their physical attractiveness. The reason: Everyone has their own definition of what attractive is.

For example, I was once set up on a date by a friend of mine with a girl who he swore up and down was attractive—I didn't agree at all. On another occasion, I had a relative set me up with a girl who said that she was just fair looking—but had a "great personality." Well, I'm here to tell you that not only did she have a great personality, but that she was far from fair. She was an absolute knockout by my standards. Starting to get my drift? Get substantive information about who that person is—not physical information about how they look. You be the judge of that on your own. Don't have expectations and you'll have nothing that can be lowered or heightened. It'll just be.

In addition, you should come up with a game plan. Have an idea in mind of where you'd like to go out with that person and when you're available to get together. Have a game plan B if they're unable to accommodate your game plan A. In other words, be flexible, and have alternative days and places you can get together. Take into consideration where they live and where you live. Don't make someone you're asking out drive an hour to see you. Generally, it's best to meet halfway.

Also, depending on your age and location—be careful about which day of the week you select to go out. Young adults—meaning people in their early to mid-twenties—sometimes don't like blind dating on the weekend—they'd rather go out with their friends to a bar. This is especially true in major urban centers like Los Angeles, New York, Chicago, and Miami. As people get older, they like bars less and less, and are more willing to date on weekends. In essence, think carefully about whether your game plan includes a weekday or weekend night. You be the judge.

In this book, I usually don't go into where to go on dates and what to do on dates—that's another book in and of itself.

However, I will tell you that on your first date, blind or other, I highly recommend keeping it simple. Rarely have I taken someone out for a big meal on my first date. It's unnecessary and it gets expensive—especially if you're dating two or three times a week.

In both my personal life and with my clients, I have found that meeting for drinks at a nice bar or lounge is the best way to meet someone on a first date—I've even gone on walks with people the first time I've met them. As you will read later in this book, I don't recommend bars as places to meet new people to date. However, I do recommend them as date spots—especially during the week when they're not swarmed and the music isn't blaring so that you can't have a conversation. In a bar, during the week, two people can have a glass of wine and have a nice conversation. If you're not a drinker, choose a cool coffee shop with some atmosphere to meet at. Again, reserve the big expensive dinner. You can offer that on a second or third date.

Also, remember to be friendly and confident. It will come across on the phone. In Step 3, I'll discuss proper conversation when you meet new people. You can and should utilize these techniques in introductory phone calls as well. For example, you should never talk about your income or past relationships with a new potential companion. That *should* be a given, but sadly, many people just don't get it. On that first phone call all you need is a pleasant demeanor, a good sense of humor, and confidence—the rest is gravy.

Also, don't wait too long to call. Once you've obtained their contact information, don't wait three weeks to contact a blind date. Chances are they're curious about you and the more you delay, the more you give them an impression of you being a flaky person. Always act sooner than later. While perhaps contacting the person that same day will appear to be too anxious, you should make a move at least within a couple of days of getting the number or e-mail address.

Finally, the Contactor should always call the Contacted the day before they are scheduled to get together to confirm. Why? Well, for one, people sometimes forget. Second, you will want to get a sense of how to identify them when you meet up. Ask them what color their hair is. How tall are they? What will they be wearing? Give them a specific place to meet you.

WHEN YOU'RE THE CONTACTED

The Contacted is the person who simply needs to wait and see if the Contactor will make contact. For instance, remember Dana from earlier in this chapter. Her mother had given her phone number out to Saul Burgerstein. In that scenario, Saul was the Contactor, and Dana was the Contacted.

So what should you do if you're going to be contacted? Just like the Contactor, try to find out as much about the person calling you as you can from your intermediary. Remember, substantive, not physical.

Just like the Contactor, you should be confident and friendly on the phone, if not more so. Remember, this person had the guts to pick up the phone or send an e-mail to a complete stranger—for a lot of people, this isn't easy. Try to be as receptive to them as you'd want them to be to you, if you were the Contactor.

In addition, don't expect everyone to have a game plan A or

be good at the initial contact. Remember, not everyone has read my book—and not everyone, like you, will be an expert on what to do. Don't hold it against them. Don't be judgmental if they don't seem to have it all together on the first call. If they don't have a game plan A, work with them, and figure out a time and place to meet that is convenient for both of you. As you'll see later in this book, it's important to learn to improvise. That goes for walking up to someone on the street and for conversations with blind dates.

THE INITIAL CONVERSATION

The following is an example of a solid first phone call between Jody and Neal. Jody's mother met Neal at a wedding. Jody is the Contactor and Neal is the Contacted. Closely follow the rhythms and changes in the conversation.

"Hello," Neal says as he answers the phone.

"Hi, Neal, this is Jody Blackwell. My mother said you'd be expecting my call," Jody says.

"Hey Jody," Neal replies. "Yes, I was expecting your call. How's your Mom doing?"

"Thanks for asking. She's great," Jody says. "You know, typical mother setting her daughter up on a blind date."

Neal laughs.

"I know what you're saying," Neal responds. "My mother does the same thing. I'm thinking about setting her up with somebody. She got divorced last year. I think it's time for a little payback."

Jody laughs.

"Great idea," Jody says. "Let me know her reaction. So, my mother says that you two were introduced at a wedding. She said that you were really nice and to top it off, a great dancer."

"You're mother is too kind," Neal said. "She must like break dancing."

Jody laughs.

"So, I was thinking maybe we could get together for a drink next Thursday night at this great new place on 2nd Avenue that just opened," Jody says.

"Next Thursday is a bad night for me," Neal says. "Are you free on Wednesday?"

"I am," Jody says.

"Great," Neal says. "You're mother told me a lot about you. I can't wait to put a face with the voice."

"Me either," Jody says. "And perhaps you'll show me some of your moves on the dance floor sometime."

"I'll do my best," Neal says. "My back is still recovering from doing the worm at the wedding."

They both have a chuckle.

"I'll call you next Tuesday to confirm and tell you how to find me once we're there," Jody says. "Talk to you then."

"Next Tuesday," Neal says. "Bye."

"Bye," Jody replies.

The initial conversation can be just this short or you can choose to make it longer. This particular example is just to give you an idea of how easy it is to set up a date with someone you've never met before. Let's examine some of the dialogue:

- Jody reminded Neal who she was by announcing her full name, "Jody Blackwell," and how she came to call him. If she had just said Jody, it may have taken Neal a minute to figure out who exactly he was talking to. Instead, Jody confidently reminded him who she was and how the phone call came to be. Remember, if someone gives you contact information for a blind date, it's better to call sooner than later.

- Jody doesn't hide the issue that she's calling Neal for a blind date. In fact, she states, "You know, typical mother, setting her daughter up on a blind date." Remember, there's no shame in blind dating. We all do it. Therefore, it's better to just be upfront about the awkwardness of blind dating. Jody was smart and she did this in a humorous way—by joking about her "typical mother." Honesty is the best approach. Embrace the awkwardness; don't try to cover it up. Use it to your advantage in a humorous way—it shows confidence.

- Jody had a game plan A. She had an idea of where and when she would like to get together with Neal. She was specific with a time and place. Doing this shows forethought and confidence. Even if someone can't make that exact time, they'll take notice that you know what you want and how to go about it—which can be a very attractive quality. Another fine quality is being flexible. Jody did what I described and was flexible to Neal's alternative evening—or as we say, game plan B.

- Jody told Neal she would call him the night before the scheduled date to confirm their meeting. A very smart move. People do forget and it's important if you're the

initiator, whether in your personal or business life, to confirm plans. Further, Neal probably has never seen a picture
of Jody, so he won't be able to identify her if she doesn't
give him a description of what she looks like and what
she's wearing on that day.

- The entire conversation was light, humorous, a little silly,
  and short. You can choose to extend a conversation or not.
  Really, it doesn't matter. However, don't talk so much on
  the first phone call or prior to the date, that when you get
  on the date, you feel you've exhausted subjects to talk
  about on the date. A conversation expert may never run
  out of things to talk about. However, you may not be an
  expert yet and may want to reserve your big questions for
  the day that you actually meet.

Now that we've gone through an example of a telephone call,
let's go through an e-mail scenario. It's the information age and
people are communicating more and more through cyberspace.
E-mail is an easy way to get a dialogue going and quite possibly
may be the only information your intermediary gives you.

The following e-mail is from Todd to Janie. Todd has never
met his intermediary—meaning, Janie is a friend of a friend of a
friend. Todd's friend got Janie's e-mail address through his
friend, and then gave it to Todd.

Dear Janie:

*Hi. How are you? My name is Todd Sellers. My friend
Jim, who's friends with your friend Tracy, said that you'd
be expecting my e-mail. Jim mentioned that Tracy said*

*that you lived in Houston, and that you went to Tulane
University. I did as well. I graduated in 1994. When did
you graduate? Maybe we know some more people in
common. Would you like to grab a drink with me later
this week? I know a great bar where we can get away
from the smog. Hope all is well.*

Todd

Simple, right? Let's take a look at what Todd wrote:

- Todd told Janie who he was and how he was connected to
  her. Of course, Janie was probably expecting Todd to write,
  but it's still a good idea to refresh someone's memory.

- Todd used the fact that he went to Tulane University as a
  connection. This is something I like to refer to as a Comfort
  Connection. When people have something in common with
  other people, especially places they've lived, schools they've
  attended, and mutual friends, they feel more at ease. It's
  comforting to know that at the very least, you can always
  refer to that common bond for a laugh or a memory during a discussion.

- You'll notice how Todd didn't have a game plan A. Why?
  Well, because e-mail isn't interactive with the other person.
  They have to read it—then respond. Therefore, it's unnecessary to suggest a time and a place before the other person
  has responded. As a matter of fact, if Todd did include a
  game plan A in the e-mail, it would come off poorly. The
  skills required for writing an e-mail and having a phone
  conversation are slightly different. With an e-mail you

must realize that the other person cannot hear your voice, cannot respond at that point in time, and cannot hear intonations in your voice. Be careful about how forceful or weak you come across in writing e-mails. Simply be courteous, confident, and respectful.

- Todd used humor. If you know anything about Houston, you know that it's covered in smog. It's an obvious joke to everyone who lives in Houston. Be clever, but not too clever. Get to the point, use a little humor, and you'll be on your way.

Let's take a look at Janie's response:

Todd:

Hey! Great to hear from you. Yes, Tracy told me that you'd be e-mailing. I'm excited to hear from another Tulane grad. I graduated after you—in 1998—I'm just a baby. I miss school. Wasn't it great? So, I'd love to meet up with you and talk about people we know, school, etc. Perhaps Thursday night? If that's good for you, just let me know the time and place and I'll be there. Looking forward to getting out of the smog. Yuck! Hope to hear from you soon.

Janie

See how warm and friendly Janie was? She was also smart. She used Todd's Comfort Connection, relayed that she graduated later than him, and then said she'd love to meet up and talk about mutual friends and school. Also, she suggests a day of the week and left it in Todd's court to choose the time and place. She met him halfway by suggesting the night. Finally, Janie built on Todd's joke about the smog. After Todd reads this e-mail, he'll have a good feeling about Janie—in that she is cool, confident, fun, and bright.

With the right perspective, blind dating can be relatively painless. It can also serve as a tool for building your interpersonal skills, as you learn to go on dates with less information than you would have if you met someone face to face. Blind dating can also be looked at as practice, as you build up your experience within the dating world. Although some of the blind dates you're set up on may not be great successes, try to keep in mind that each bad date carries its own positive learning experience. As Cameron Crowe wrote in his movie *Vanilla Sky*, "The sweet is never as sweet, without the sour."

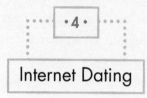

Internet Dating

I want to tell you a story about a former client of mine, Steven. When I first met Steven, he lived in Los Angeles. He was a great guy, but very timid and wasn't good at approaching women. Sure, he occasionally met girls. After all, he was a handsome man, but not terribly confident in himself. But in Los Angeles's dating scene, shyness is not rewarded. Los Angeles is filled with Type A personalities—people are aggressive, a bit self-absorbed, and impressed with power. It is a tough place for anyone to date, much less Steven.

As Steven approached his mid-twenties, he got tired of being timid and came to me for help. Unfortunately, we didn't have a lot of time together to work one on one, because soon after I met him, he returned to New York to attend graduate school on Long Island. Steven was sure his dating life would improve once he moved back to Long Island, but, it turned out to be even more of a drag.

Steven found himself spending long hard days by himself, isolated and studying. It turned out that the graduate school he attended left a lot to be desired in the female department and therefore wasn't going to be a source for many dates. And even when Steven did have the opportunity to go out, he went to bars—a nightmare for the shy guy. Steven's location had changed, but his basic problem hadn't—he was lonely and still wasn't good at meeting women.

About a month after Steven had started school, I received a phone call from him. He was upset. He'd been on Long Island for nearly a month and outside of the few girls that he wasn't attracted to at his school, he had zero female contact. "Drive into Manhattan," I told him. "Walk the streets, go into stores, and talk to women." "David, you know I'm not good at that," he said. "I know you've taught me to be more assertive, but it just comes so hard for me. Maybe we didn't get enough time to work together one on one."

At this point, I realized that I needed to come up with an idea specifically tailored to cure Steven's anxiety, shyness, and lack of assertiveness. I needed to figure out a way to help him demystify the opposite sex—to help understand how easy it is to meet people. I also needed to figure out a way to do this from across the country.

For the next several days, I racked my brain for an idea. One afternoon, I was watching a television show about the military—specifically, what new recruits had to endure during basic training, or as they call it, boot camp. Suddenly, it hit me. I came up with the idea of Boot Camp Internet Dating.

In the military, when new recruits come in, they have no idea how to be soldiers. However, within months, they are considered ready to go off to war. Steven needed to go through the same type of intense training that new recruits went through— once he did, like the soldiers, he would be ready to take on any challenge. Exposing Steven to an onslaught of dates in a short amount of time would accomplish several objectives. First, it would take the pressure off of him to succeed on every date, as if that date was the only one he'd have for the next six months. Second, by exposing him to a rigorous dating schedule it would improve his interpersonal communication skills by allowing him to see himself in numerous scenarios with many different personalities in a short, compacted amount of time. Third, throughout those numerous dates, he may actually find someone whose company he enjoys and wants to continue spending time with. If not, by the end of the boot camp, he'd at the very least build up new skills that would serve him in the future. I was confident, like a solider, he would be ready to take on any challenge to come his way.

There was one last detail to figure out—how he'd get all of those dates in a short amount of time. Where was there a pool of single people to choose from where Steven didn't have to walk up to and start a conversation? The Internet! That was the answer. I went online, typed Steven's area code into one of the large Internet dating services, and found a bevy of attractive, interesting girls who lived near Steven and were looking for a guy just like him. I called him immediately.

"Steven," I said. "I want you to go on the Internet, put up a profile on an Internet dating service, and e-mail ten women tonight."

"Internet dating?" Steven said horrified. "No way. That's for desperate people."

"Steven," I said. "Listen to me. You paid me to help you. For your own benefit, listen to my advice. I know what I'm doing."

"What are you doing?" Steven asked me.

"Just do what I tell you and when you've completed my task, you'll understand the point of the exercise," I said confidently. "Try to think of the movie *The Karate Kid*. I'm Mr. Miyagi. You're Daniel-son. No questions, just act."

At first, Steven was reluctant. In fact, for the next three days all he did was contemplate it. What if someone he knew saw him on the Internet? Would they think he was a loser? Isn't the Internet a last resort? Mind you, this was several years ago, before the Internet exploded as a source for singles to meet one another. Many people at that time were still worried about how they would be perceived and what it actually meant to date via cyberspace.

As luck would have it, Steven came home after an evening out with his graduate school buddies—and a bottle of Jack Daniel's—to an empty apartment. Again, he'd met no women. Hearing my voice in his head, Steven sat on his sofa staring at his computer. As the story was told to me, he slowly stood up, stumbled over to the computer, turned it on, sat down, and signed into cyberspace. He typed "online dating" into a search engine and began to browse the different online dating sites, happening upon the site I had suggested to him. He whipped out his credit card and signed up. Next, he filled out a profile and uploaded a picture of himself. Then, he began going through the multitude of profiles of women in his area. As he searched, he found many attractive women who had interesting things to say about themselves and what they were looking for in a partner.

Well, as legend has it, Steven didn't send out just one e-mail that evening. He didn't even send out ten like I'd encouraged him to. No, he spent the next three hours sending out twenty e-mails to twenty different women.

The next morning, when Steven woke up, he couldn't believe what he'd done. Lying in bed hungover, he ducked under his blanket—one part of his brain trying to remember where he'd put the aspirin, the other part in disbelief at what he'd done the night before. After a half hour, he finally decided to get out of bed and check his e-mail. When he did, he found that already four of the twenty women he'd contacted answered him back. He was shocked. One by one, he read through their e-mails, each one saying that they liked his profile and picture and wanted to know more about him. He was in awe. It was as if suddenly an entire world opened up to him at the click of a button. In his entire life, meeting women had never been that easy.

For the next hour, Steven reexamined each woman's profile, taking a closer look at what they had to say. He then made a list of each girl's name, profile number, e-mail address, and little bits of information to distinguish them so he wouldn't get confused. One by one, he responded to the women's e-mails. By the end of the day, he'd set up four dates—one for each night of the rest of the week. "That's crazy," you may think. Remember, there were still sixteen e-mails yet to be answered.

Over the next week, one e-mail after another rolled into Steven's inbox. During the next two and a half weeks, Steven ended up going out with sixteen women—almost a different woman every night. It was a formidable task for any man, much less the timid Steven. As the result of years of frustration and longing, Steven seized upon his new array of options with vigor. After the two and half weeks were over and he'd gone out with every girl, he called me.

"Mr. Miyagi," Steven said. "I now understand what you were trying to accomplish by getting me to browse the Internet."

"Good, Daniel-son," I said. "Please tell Miyagi your story."

"Over the past two and half weeks, I dated sixteen of the twenty girls I e-mailed," Steven said. "Four of them I had no physical chemistry with, but they were really nice. Four of them I had physical chemistry with, but they weren't so nice. Four of them weren't interested in me. But it doesn't matter because out of the initial sixteen, I have second dates lined up with the remaining four."

"And what have you learned from this?" I asked.

"I learned that I'm getting really good at dating," Steven said joyfully. "It was intense. I learned so much from going out with those girls. The way people behave, the way I behave. Also, I didn't feel any pressure to succeed. I knew if a date went bad, I had another one the next night. As a result, I could be more myself. The neon sign of desperation on my forehead you always talk about disappeared. I feel so much more confident. Like I could talk to anyone or go on a date with anyone right now and be cool and in control. Not to mention, and this is the best part—yesterday, when I was at the supermarket, I saw this really cute girl and walked right up to her and introduced myself. We're going out next week. Can you believe that?"

"I'm proud of you, Steven," I said. "You took initiative and had the confidence to put yourself out there. Now, you're reaping the rewards. This change is a process that you must continually nurture. Always be open. Become a sponge to the signs the world and people are sending you—observe, listen, and you'll be a master communicator and eventually a master dater. Although it sounds like you're well on your way already."

"Thank you for the advice, Mr. Miyagi," Steven said.

"Thank you for proving me right, Daniel-son," I said. "Now, go paint the fence."

There are some important lessons you should take from Steven's story. By Boot Camp Internet Dating, you're releasing the pressure from yourself to succeed and as a result, are more likely to just be yourself. You won't be putting on a show—because frankly, you know there are more dates waiting in queue. Sound coldhearted? It's not, it's life. There are literally millions of people out there who go on a date once every three weeks, a month, or even a year. If a person is waiting that long in anticipation of that date, you don't have to wonder what kind of pressure they are putting onto themselves to succeed on that date.

You can't wait around your entire life for that one date, hoping it will be the one to change the course of your life. It's insanity. Instead, you have to go out and aggressively get dates for yourself so that you don't have to spend your life waiting for that once-a-season date. People who go into a date in desperation reek of it. Take the pressure off by Boot Camp Internet Dating.

Another important lesson is that Steven unconsciously became a more observant and introspective dater. What he was evaluating was in fact himself within several dating scenarios and the behavior of those he was with. If a date went well, he sat down and thought about why. If one of Steven's dates didn't go well, he thought about why it didn't go well. There were times, after an honest self-evaluation, that he figured out that a date hadn't gone well because of his own behavior. Sometimes, he found that a date went poorly because of the other person's behavior. At other times, there simply wasn't chemistry and it was no one's fault. Remember, the goal during our journey isn't just to find dates, it's to become more in tune with other people and ourselves, so that when the right person does come along, you're equipped with the skills to handle it.

Like Steven, as a result of your Boot Camp Internet Dating, you will become more confident going up to people on the street. Steven went up to the woman in the grocery store and soon, if you follow my advice, you'll be able to do something similar. Again, while Boot Camp Internet Dating, you're not only improving your interpersonal communication skills, but you're also releasing the pressure on yourself to always succeed while simultaneously searching for someone you like, and building confidence.

After Steven went through a course of Boot Camp Internet Dating, it suddenly dawned on him that it really was just that easy to meet new people to date. He was feeling on top of the world. He had four dates set up with girls that were interested in him—no one was going to knock him down. That's precisely the attitude you need to have in order to succeed. Even if Steven had gotten rejected by the girl in the grocery store, he knew he had four dates lined up later that week with women who were interesting, attractive, and interested in him.

Over the next several weeks, Steven continued to date two of the women he'd met while simultaneously sending out more e-mails, receiving new ones, and setting up new dates. Sometimes he ended up with one-night stands, sometimes with someone he would date frequently, sometimes with nothing at all—but he enjoyed the ride of self-exploration and the exploration of the opposite sex.

Steven didn't get depressed if he got rejected and didn't think he was a deity if he'd succeeded. He studied his behavior and others' behavior and learned to adapt to his situations and environment in a very skilled way—like a chameleon. He learned how to make people comfortable, how to relax them with humor, and how to make them feel attractive at the right moments. He figured out how to stir up emotions in them that other men with their flashy clothes and cars, and endless bantering about their success and money, didn't know how to do. He learned to take an interest in women and what they had to say.

As a result, I'm happy to say that Steven has a girlfriend that he's been with for almost two years and he's very much in love. How many dates did it take him to find her? According to Steve, over the course of graduate school, probably close to 150. Yet, he said it was a fun journey and worth it just to find her.

The skills that Steven picked up through Boot Camp Internet Dating can only be learned by trial and error and honest self-evaluation. While I can give you the outline as I am doing in this book, you must be willing to go out there, look, listen, and learn from both your successes and mistakes. Do you have to schedule sixteen dates in two weeks? No. However, in the beginning, I suggest you line up at least three dates a week via the Internet. If used in conjunction with blind dating and meeting people about town, it won't take long until you feel as if you can handle any dating situation.

FINDING A WEBSITE FOR YOU

There are hundreds of online dating sites. Yahoo Personals, Lavalife, and Date.com are among the biggest. Other, more specific sites like Jdate.com, cater to a more specific client base such as Jewish singles. All one has to do is go to a search engine such as Yahoo or Google, type in "online dating," or something more specific such as "Catholic online dating" and you will find a dating site that meets your needs.

Once you sign up with a service, the first thing you'll have to do is create a profile. Every website has different questions that you must answer in your profile. Some questions are broad, such as: What are you looking for in a date? Other questions, are specific, such as: If you could be any animal, what kind would you be? How you answer these questions is up to you. However, I must caution you that your profile is your calling card. It's one of the first things that a potential date will see if they're searching the database for dates, and the second thing they'll see if you e-mail them first. Therefore, I strongly urge you to take time planning out how you'll answer these questions. When you're done answering them, I also urge you to have a friend review it for you and ask them what they think of the content, spelling, and grammar. Potential dates are generally not attracted to illiterates or people too lazy to make a good first impression—unless of course, they take the same lax approach you do.

CREATING YOUR PROFILE

On most dating sites, the first thing someone will see when browsing for dates is your picture and subject line. If your subject line and picture catches someone's eye, they'll be drawn in further, click on your profile, and read it. Some dating sites give you several questions to answer. Some of these questions are open ended and some have choices that you simply check off.

In regard to the questions with choices, the answers you select are up to you and should honestly reflect who you are. However, there's one question that appears on many Internet dating sites that I have a problem with people answering—the question about your annual income.

I believe that how much money you make is personal and is something that should only be talked about with another person once you've become intimate, so it's not something for you to broadcast to the entire world. It's tacky and draws attention to you in the wrong way. Some people who answer this question feel that they need to because they're insecure about other more important qualities. They feel that if they broadcast how much money they make, they'll be more appealing to the opposite sex.

I'm still not sure why so many Internet dating sites post this question. Most people choose not to answer it anyway. However, there are still those who do, and I'd recommend staying away from them. Your income is unimportant for the purposes of finding a first date. As I stated before, if later you feel that the person you're seeing won't be able to engage in the type of lifestyle you would like because of their income, it's then that you will have a choice to make. However, remember, you don't know if the teacher who makes $30,000 a year has a trust fund or the Wall Street executive who claims he's worth millions is about to declare bankruptcy. For the purpose of meeting new people to date, these questions are better left to later when a relationship is unfolding.

In regard to the open-ended questions, you should spend quite a bit of time perfecting your answers. I recommend first drafting your answers in a word-processing program. Only after they've been reviewed, revised, and corrected should you cut and paste them into your profile. Take your time—make a great first impression. Below, I'll show you the difference between making a so-so or even bad impression and a good one.

THE OPEN-ENDED QUESTIONS

The open-ended questions give you the opportunity to impress people with your wit, experiences, and character. If you take time to answer them properly, it will enhance your ability to draw in readers and dates. In preparation for this section, I examined numerous Internet dating Websites and explored the many different types of open-ended questions that people are asked to answer for their profiles. Below are hypothetical questions I developed based on the survey that I conducted. For each question, you'll first read a bad example, and then a good one. Carefully, study the difference between the two.

Question #1: What's your idea of a good time?
Bad Example—Male Response

> I like to go out at night to bars with my friends. I watch lots of sports. I travel. I read. I watch movies on my DVD player. I listen to music.

Question #1: What's your idea of a good time?

Good Example—Male Response

Like many people in their late 20s, I work hard. However, my philosophy is if you work hard, you have to play equally hard. On the weekends, I'll grab some of my friends who are still single, and we'll check out lounges that have a cool vibe and laid-back scene. I'm not really into the club scene anymore like I was in my early 20s—I'm more into kicking back with a vodka tonic, having a good meal, and enjoying people's company. After a late Saturday night, I'll settle into my couch on Sunday afternoon and watch my favorite team, the New York Giants. I know they've been on a losing streak—but I'm hoping if I keep watching them it'll be good luck and they'll start winning again. When I'm not working, lounging, or watching the Giants, I like to travel. I'm currently planning a trip to Brazil and Argentina. Until now, I've spent most of my vacations in Europe—I'm obsessed with its history, beauty, and people. However, I'm now looking forward to seeing other places and reading about them. Reading, to me, is a total release. My favorite authors are Wally Lamb, John Updike, and Norman Mailer. If you haven't read them, I'll loan you my favorite books. I also love watching movies and listening to music. Some of my favorite movies are *Casablanca, Goodfellas*, and *Airplane!*. As for music, anything goes. I'm open minded. I'll listen to anything from John Coltrane to Metallica. I have an iPod and take it everywhere I go.

Do you see the difference between the bad example and the good example? How much more did we learn about the personality of the author of the second response as opposed to the first? In the bad example, we simply get a vague picture of who that person is. Anyone could write the bad example—it's generic. However, in the good example, we get a sense of who this person is, his likes, what matters to him most, and how he spends the days of his life. It's also specific as to where he likes to travel, his favorite authors, movies, and musicians. These are catch words that will appeal to someone who is browsing and has the same interests. Also, he threw in some humor about his favorite team—the New York Giants. People love to laugh. If you can write something funny, then by all means go for it. Humor is an extremely appealing and attractive quality in a person—utilize it where possible, but only if you're confident it's funny. Let's look at another question.

Question # 2: Where do you like to frequent and what are your favorite travel destinations?
Bad Response—Female

> Club Cameo, Chill, Vapid, Water's Edge Restaurant, and the coffee shop on my corner—Willy's. As for travel destinations, Spain, Las Vegas, and the Napa Valley.

Question #2: Where do you like to frequent and what are your favorite travel destinations?
Good Response—Female

> This question gives me the choice of answering one or the other—but I'll answer both so you can get a better idea of

what I enjoy. There's a blues bar called Club Cameo that not many people really know about. A coworker of mine once took me there. Amazing. Every Wednesday night, old men get up on stage for four hours straight and jam out the best old blues tunes—occasionally, and this is the best part, they will improvise and bring people up on stage. I was chosen once and came up with two lines. It was so much fun. I also love the bar Chill, because the inside looks like an ice box. It's got that *A Clockwork Orange* feel to it. Makes you feel like you're in the year 2050. Sometimes I'll go to Vapid—but only for an hour—just long enough so we can watch all the people with attitudes size each other up and talk nasty about one another. It gives me and my girlfriends a good laugh. At least once a month, I'll check out the Water's Edge Restaurant. The oysters there are to die for, the bar scene is hot, and the people are friendly. I don't know if a coffee shop qualifies as a hot spot, but on Saturday afternoon I go to Willy's, sit outside, and read the paper. There's a great outdoor patio, the coffee is Tanzanian (YUM), and they give free refills.

Part Two—Travel. Spain, Spain, Spain, and more Spain. I spent a semester in Madrid in college and loved every second of it. I made some friends there and go back at least once a year to visit, drink Sangria, and dance until seven in the morning. I also frequent Las Vegas. I'll admit, I have an itch for blackjack. My father taught me to play when I was a kid. I only play five dollar hands, but I'm hypnotized by it. I'll play for hours. And finally, I love the

Napa Valley. It's gorgeous. I love wine so it's a real treat for me to go from one vineyard to the next. You get to keep the wine glasses too.

Again, do you see the difference? Don't just list off places that you like, tell us why you like them. Give the reader an idea of who you are, what you like, and why you like it.

The following bad example is an example of what I referred to earlier in the book as a rigid list person—a person who writes qualifications as if they're an employer looking to hire an employee—I've come across many of these and more are from women than men. The bad example comes from someone so particular, so high maintenance, that they have a very difficult time finding dates because frankly, no one could possibly ever live up to their standards.

Question #3: Who are you and who do you want to meet?
Bad Example—Female

I'm tall, thin, and beautiful. I expect the same in a man. I'm Ivy league educated and I expect a man to be the same. If you aren't a lawyer, doctor, accountant, or a top executive at a corporation—do not respond to my profile. If you're not between 6'1 and 6'3, please don't waste my time. If you're over 200lbs, go lose some weight, and again, don't waste my time. You must also have dark hair, dark features, and blue eyes. You can't be hairy either. I hate hairy men. You must take care of your skin, be clean cut and dress fashionably. I'm a princess and I expect to be treated as such. You should always open doors for me and pull out my chair. I like presents too. If you are bad in bed, don't apply. If you've slept with more than 10 women, don't apply. If your parents are divorced, don't apply. If you're not a practicing Catholic who attends church regularly, don't waste my time. All of this may seem particular to you, but the person who fits this profile will understand. I like what I like, so don't waste my time or yours either.

Question #3: Who are you and who do you want to meet?
Good Example—Female

I would say I'm attractive—at least my mother tells me I'm beautiful and occasionally a man on the street will give me a cat call. I'm tall, about 5'10. I work out a lot so I consider myself to be in pretty good shape. I have long brown hair and I think my best features are my eyes. I'm laid back—although occasionally at work I get a little high strung—but nothing that a good glass of wine and some good music can't relax me from. I'm looking for someone who has similar interests to my own, however, I'm open to new places, thoughts, and ideas. I'm always willing to learn. Physically, my ideal man would be around 6'1, tall, dark, and handsome. However, I love personality and if you've got it, you could be 5'6 and blonde. I love to laugh—so please have a good sense of humor. Life is too short to be serious all the time. I guess I'd say I'm a girl who likes the finer things in life, but at the same time can go to a bar in jeans and a T-shirt and watch baseball games.

Wow! Do you see the difference here? You may think that the bad example is completely fabricated, but it's not. As a matter of fact, I've even seen worse. There are actually people out there who write gibberish like that. These rigid list–type of people are so demanding that it's unlikely they'll ever find a companion— no one could possibly live up to those standards. In essence, she has narrowed her search to a wealthy, Ivy League educated, celibate, Pierce Brosnan type. I wish her the best of luck.

When working on your profile, keep in mind that we all have an idea of how we see ourselves and what we want in another person. In your profile, try to emphasize the interesting and positive attributes you possess, but don't be afraid to poke fun at yourself, either. Self-deprecating humor is endearing. Also, when you describe what you're looking for in a companion, don't be too rigid. Only list qualities that are the most important to you and be careful what you choose. For instance, it may be important to you that your companion has an appreciation for music. That's fine. Say that. However, I'd never say that you only like men who are Ivy League educated. Why narrow yourself? Trust me, there are plenty of people out there who didn't go to an Ivy league school who are every bit as smart as someone who did. Hence, be broad enough to encompass a large group of men and women, but be specific enough, in a gentle way, so people know that you have certain tastes without coming off as a shallow person.

SENDING OUT E-MAILS

Now that you're done with your profile, I suggest browsing the database of profiles to find people who appeal to you. Everyone has different taste, but keep in mind that nobody's perfect and no profile can encompass all the facets of a human being.

While browsing, the first thing you will be attracted to will be somebody's photograph. A word of caution, photographs can be deceiving. Some photographs make people look better than they really are and some photographs make people look more unattractive than they really are. Sometimes, if you click on a profile there will be more than one photograph. Although physical attraction and chemistry are important, I recommend that if you see a photograph of someone you find only mildly attractive, to explore their profile in more depth. You never know what you'll find.

Inside the profile, you should carefully examine what people write in their answers. Ask yourself how much, if any, thought they put into it. Have they thoroughly answered the questions? Although it's inconclusive, someone who puts no effort into their own profile is either just plain lazy or doesn't really care about being on the service and is just testing the waters. Either way, it's not a good sign. Why would you want to go out with a person who is still lukewarm about meeting someone on the Internet? They may eventually freak out and dump you because they get the image in their head of being at their wedding and having to tell people they met their new wife or husband in cyberspace. Although silly in this modern age, some people just aren't comfortable with it yet. Go for the people that are eager to meet you—the one's who are putting themselves out there and opening up.

Once you find a profile you like, the next step is to write to them. Women shouldn't be shy about e-mailing a man first. Remember what we talked about in Step 1—women must break tradition. You're going to get aggressive with your search for companionship.

When you zone in on a person you want to meet, you must craft an e-mail. My advice: Keep it short and sweet. Let your profile do the talking and serve as your calling card. There's no need to write a novel to someone the first time you contact them. It reeks of desperation and the smell isn't pretty. I have collected a tremendous amount of data in this area.

Men, more than women, tend to write too much. There have been reported cases where men have written up to three-page letters introducing themselves. I have even heard of men proposing marriage from foreign countries on a first e-mail. I can only imagine how they act when meeting someone in person. These are what I call Delusional Romantics—people who think that they can act like they're in a movie and get others to respond. It just doesn't work that way in reality. The majority of things we see people do for romance in a movie never work in reality. In movies it's cute and sweet; in reality it's frightening and shows a lack of social skills.

When writing, it's much more appealing to write something brief—it shows you're confident in your profile. Your e-mail should simply introduce yourself, compliment them on their profile, and request them to look at yours. If they're interested, they'll write back. If they don't write back, don't be offended. Everybody's taste is different—it's not about you.

For instance, let's say you told a woman she had to choose a date between Tom Cruise and George Clooney, and she chose Tom Cruise. Do you think that another woman, put in the same situation wouldn't choose George Clooney? Should George be upset that Tom was chosen over him? No. Next time around, it may be George's turn. Different strokes for different folks. As long as you're polite in your introduction, you have nothing to be ashamed of or if someone doesn't respond to your e-mail. This especially goes for men.

Men must realize that many attractive women they e-mail on Internet dating sites get inundated inboxes. I once had a beautiful female client who posted her profile and the first day she received 150 e-mails. She was so overwhelmed that she signed off the service and didn't e-mail anyone back. Be patient. If your profile is good, you'll get responses.

Below is an example of a simple letter that you can use if you'd like. Obviously, you should vary this a little bit, but feel free to use my words:

Dear Jessica:

Hi. I was just browsing the profiles on Yahoo Personals and I came across yours. Your picture is adorable and I liked what you had to say in the answers to the questions. I think we may have a lot in common. Check out my profile and if you agree, drop me an e-mail. Hope to hear from you soon.

John

Short and sweet, right? Jessica will appreciate the fact that John hasn't taken up twenty minutes of her day with a three-page e-mail. Instead, she'll simply click on John's profile, look at his picture, look at his answers, and if John matches what she's looking for, he'll receive an e-mail back. It's that simple. No mystery at all. Really! You should never feel like you have to coerce someone into going out with you—especially on the Internet. There are far too many singles online to waste your time with someone who isn't interested. If your profile is strong, plenty of people will be attracted to it and will want to date you. Sell yourself, but never oversell yourself. Promote yourself through the subtext of what you write. You don't have to say, "Hi, I'm a nice guy." Simply write something nice. Get it?

WHAT TO DO WHEN SOMEONE WRITES YOU

It doesn't matter whether you write someone first or they write you first, the point is, you've made contact with someone new. From here on in, it's up to you to be diligent and follow up in order to turn making contact into making a date. You have a few choices. First, there is the most aggressive approach, which would be to get their phone number. Let's say Jessica wrote John back with this letter:

Dear John:

Hi. I received your e-mail. Thanks for writing me. I checked out your profile and I think you're right, we do have some things in common. Not to mention, you're pretty adorable yourself.

Jessica

John has an array of choices. My favorite move—get the phone number right off the bat. I don't see any reason to sit and trade e-mails for two weeks before talking to someone on the phone. The longer you draw out the anticipated phone call the more pressure you're putting on yourself—and as you know we don't want pressure. I recommend John writing back the following:

Dear Jessica:

Great to hear back from you. If you're comfortable with it, send me your phone number and I'll give you a call this evening around nine o'clock. Looking forward to putting the voice with the face.

John

Simple! Later that night John can call Jessica up and they can get to know each other on the phone. Then, at the end of that conversation, John should ask Jessica out for a date. Like blind dating, John should have a game plan A—where and when he would like to meet Jessica. He should also have a game plan B just in case Jessica can't get together at that time. Remember, flexibility is key.

If you decide not to go for the phone number right off the bat or they don't want to provide you with their number, your other options are to continue to e-mail or instant message with a person a few times before asking them for their phone number. I've done some great flirting via instant message and e-mail, and so have my clients—but writing one e-mail after another can become time consuming and annoying. We're all busy people and you can learn a lot from someone by the way they communicate over the phone.

I hope this section has enlightened you about how to correctly go about dating through the Internet. The Internet is an exciting place for singles in the new millennium—it makes meeting people and setting up dates easier than ever. If up to this point in your life you've looked at the Internet as something for the desperate—think again. There are millions of healthy, normal, educated, and attractive people using the Internet as an alternative source to meet companions. Used in conjunction with blind dating and meeting people about town, you'll never fall short of dates again. Remember, always expand your dating possibilities. Use everything at your disposal—you never know where the love of your life will come from.

• 5 •

Meeting People About Town

In the previous two chapters I discussed blind dating and Internet dating, but what about the good old-fashioned, traditional way of meeting people—face to face? At last we have arrived at my favorite way to meet people—meeting people about town. To me, meeting people about town is the most challenging, exciting, and rewarding because it forces you to be creative. While meeting people about town all of your senses must be acute. You must be on your toes and open to the possibilities. It's at this point especially where the awareness and availability I spoke of in Step 1 comes into play.

I can't begin to tell you how many of my clients have come to me and told me that they simply can't meet people about town. After careful analysis, I've realized two truths. First, most of these clients don't know the right places to look for people and second, even if they did see them, they don't have the skills to bring about the desired result—contact. Fact—single people are everywhere, and I mean everywhere. This chapter will address where you can go to find single people—mainly throughout your daily routine or through your hobbies. Then in Step 3, Making Contact, I'll show you easy ways to begin and maintain conversations with people once you do find them. However, for now, let's concentrate on the infinite places and times of opportunity that surround you everyday. To do this, I'm going to tell you a story about a client of mine named Jennifer.

Jennifer lived in Miami and was an extremely successful in-house accountant for a major corporation. When I interviewed Jennifer over the phone she told me she had a fantastic job, but that she never met nice guys and didn't understand why. After listening to Jennifer for a while, I realized that she had a couple of problems.

First, it was clear that Jennifer was a passive waiter. For most of her adult life, she'd expected men to initiate contact with her. Jennifer's mother had always told her that men are supposed to make the first move. If you recall Step 1, this is also known as The Tradition Myth.

Second, as the old song goes, Jennifer was "Looking for Love in All the Wrong Places." When she wasn't at home droning on about how lonely she was, she was out with her other poorly skilled single female friends, frequenting the hippest bars on South Beach hoping to find dates for the following week. The few times she'd actually met men at these bars, they were nothing like she hoped they'd be and she went on to describe several uncomfortable situations. As a result, Jennifer was convinced that she would never find an interesting, creative, and intelligent man with whom she could share her life.

After hearing Jennifer's dilemma and agreeing to work with her, I asked her to e-mail me her typical daily routine. This is what she sent me:

David:

Today was Wednesday. On my way to work, like always, I stopped at Starbucks for coffee. At work, the first half of the day was spent doing paperwork. At lunch, a group of my coworker girlfriends and I went across the street to a local restaurant. After lunch, I ran a couple of errands. I dropped off my blouse at the dry cleaners, stopped by our subsidiary corporation to drop off some paperwork, and then I dropped film off at the one-hour photo. After the errands, I went back to work and made calls the rest of the afternoon. After work, I went to the gym, picked up dinner at the supermarket, went home, ate dinner, watched TV, and then went to sleep. Hope this helps.

Jennifer

As I read that e-mail from my house in Los Angeles, I already had images of Jennifer in Miami, clueless and unaware of the dozens of opportunities to meet people that existed within her daily routine. For the opportunities that she was aware of, I imagined her passively letting the moments float by with trepidation and her mother's mores echoing in her brain.

We're all products of our youth, and Jennifer was no

exception. Much of what happens to us in our youth stays with us through adulthood. Psychologists try to help their patients overcome faulty information or negative experiences that they fell victim to in those early years.

Although I'm not a psychologist, I work with clients in much of the same way—to help them change their behavior in the present. Unlike a psychologist though, I'll personally take a client by the hand, as opposed to sitting in an office, and show them how to change their behavior. Often, I will even travel to where a client lives so I can observe how they go about their daily routine. Observing helps me to figure the most effective way to alter their behavior. In essence, help them to realize all of the opportunities they're missing, show them how to be more aware of those opportunities, and then teach them how to seize them. In Jennifer's case, I traveled to Miami.

The evening I arrived, I met Jennifer for coffee. As is often the case with my clients, I found Jennifer to be very attractive. She dressed stylishly, had a beautiful smile, a quick wit, and a pleasing personality. From the start, I knew I wouldn't have to give her a physical makeover, just a mental one.

To get started, I asked her if I could follow her around for a day so that I could study her daily routines and interactions with others. She was surprised but curious, and supplied me with a list of her activities for the following day. The next morning, I set out to trail her.

On a Tuesday morning, I waited for Jennifer at her local Starbucks and began my observations. From my seat in the corner, I watched Jennifer walk into the store, stand on line, and order a coffee and bagel. On my little pad, I noted that there were three single men in suits also on line with her. How did I know they were single? They weren't wearing rings. Now, that doesn't mean they didn't have girlfriends, but without talking to them there was no way to know. Do you think Jennifer talked to any of them? Do you think Jennifer even noticed they were there? If you guessed yes to either question, try again.

When Jennifer left, I followed her to work in my rental car and watched her park her car. As she walked into the building, I observed an attractive man walking next to her and checking her out. It was obvious that the man wanted to talk to her but, unfortunately, Jennifer wasn't making herself available for conversation. Her arms were crossed, her sunglasses were on, and she looked miserable even if she wasn't. Her body language conveyed a very different attitude than the one I had observed the night before over coffee. I made another note in my pad.

At lunchtime, I sat in a booth at Jennifer's favorite restaurant and observed her and her friends having lunch. They were so engrossed in conversation (which happened to be about how bad their dating lives were) that they were oblivious to the six men sitting two tables down from them. Would you believe these guys were no more than ten feet away and Jennifer never once looked in their direction? I scribbled some more.

After lunch, I followed Jennifer to the bank. Standing just behind her on line was a sharply dressed, handsome gentleman. He leaned over and asked her if she had a pen he could borrow. Jennifer looked through her purse, handed the man a pen and told him to keep it. Right as the man smiled back at her and said, "Thank you," the bank teller yelled out, "Next!" Instead of noticing the sign, and striking up a conversation with the gentleman,

Jennifer turned around and went about her business. Slack-jawed, I wrote some more and already couldn't believe the number of opportunities Jennifer had missed that day.

After work that day, I observed Jennifer in the "Sweating to Techno" class at her gym. I sat back against a weight machine and chuckled to myself as she stood in between two men who both appeared to be single, and who both paid more attention to her than they did to the teacher. Think Jennifer offered to grab either one of them a mat when it was time to cool down and stretch out? Of course not.

After Jennifer's visit to the gym, I followed her to the video store and watched her look at movies in the new release section. Standing literally two feet away from her was a man looking at *When Harry Met Sally,* which—ironically—is a movie about two people who miss signs and opportunities for love. For the first time that day, I noticed Jennifer aware and taking an interest. She was craning her neck to look at the man, but because he was reading, he didn't see her. Instead of approaching him, she let him walk out of the store. At that point, I had stopped taking notes.

Our last stop was the grocery store. I watched Jennifer as she moved up and down the aisles, talking on her cell phone. At one point, I saw a man staring down the aisle at her. Of course, she never saw him and he never made a move because she was too busy yapping away to her mother in New York about the guy who didn't approach her at the video store.

When Jennifer came out of the supermarket, she found me shaking my head and chuckling at her. "Why are you laughing?" she asked. I simply pointed to the man who had looked at her, driving away in his BMW convertible and said, "You see that guy? That was a date this weekend. And it just drove off into the sunset."

Jennifer and I sat in the parking lot for the next hour. As I revealed to her everything I had observed that day, Jennifer sat speechless, envisioning all of the signs and opportunities that she had failed to seize because of her lack of awareness, her unavailability, and her passive-waiter mentality. Confronted with the mass of evidence stacked against her, Jennifer was finally willing to submit herself to a change.

Over the next week Jennifer and I spent a lot of time together, covering a lot of the territory I've hit on in the previous chapters and in the chapters to come. We acknowledged her passive tendencies, and I taught her how to be more proactive and to look more available. Equally as important, we identified all the places in her daily routine where her life automatically overlapped with the lives of other professional people who shared her interests and pastimes. Because Jennifer worked with me, I'm happy to report she's engaged to a man that she met one weekday evening at the video store. The best part of all: She initiated the conversation with him.

You can learn a lot from this anecdote. It's crucial for you to recognize how easy it is to overlook the many chances for meeting new people that may be presenting themselves on a daily basis. Try sitting down and writing out your daily routine for yourself, just as Jennifer did for me. Study it carefully. You may notice, just as Jennifer eventually did, how many opportunities are staring you boldly in the face. Become aware of those times and places in your day, and you can begin taking advantage of those opportunities. The more conscious and alert you are, the more conducive your daily routine will become to meeting someone new.

Remember the lessons from the earlier chapters, Awareness and Availability. Never lose sight of them. Write them down, put them in your purse or your wallet, and tape them to the dashboard of your car or to your computer monitor at work. Only once they've become a part of your conscious thoughts will you be able to change your faulty perceptions and behavior.

Jennifer went to a bunch of places that are great meeting spots the day I observed her, and there are many, many others. You may not have ever thought about these places as prime locations to meet other people, but trust me, they are.

Before we turn to them, I want to call your attention to the one place where you're more likely to be repeatedly frustrated and disappointed by the people you'll meet than pleasantly surprised.

the truth about bars

Ironic as it may sound, places such as bars, which we think are the best places to try to meet people, are often the worst. We dress to attract, we behave to attract, and at the same time, our defenses are up to guard against unwanted solicitations. It's virtually impossible to see the people around us as they really are. We can only see what they want us to see. More often than not, bars are a breeding ground for false advertising.

It gets worse. Remember, everyone's drinking. While there's no doubt that alcohol loosens inhibitions, it also dulls senses and clouds judgment. A few drinks into the night, and most people aren't seeing clearly. Take caution: Beer goggles follow you through your entire life. Have you ever traded numbers with a person you've met at a bar and then not remembered who they were when you spoke days later? Have you ever met for a date only to realize, to your horror, that they weren't as attractive as you'd thought, or as interesting? Let's face it. Sober encounters after an intoxicated evening have provided us all with much disappointment.

Bars are very competitive environments. In a bar, there can literally be hundreds of men going after the same woman. By the time you approach her there's a good chance she has already been suffering through the Attack of the Killer Budweisers for the last hour: the drunk frat boy, the sloppy executive, the too-smooth-for-his-own-good player, and the "How you doin'?" Joey Bag O' Doughnuts guy. Shark after shark approaches her, spewing one obnoxious line after another. By the time a nice guy such as yourself has worked up the courage to say hello, all of her defenses are up and you don't stand a chance of getting her attention, much less getting to know her. It's not too different for women. If every beauty in the bar is making eyes at the same guy, the odds just aren't in your favor, especially if you're not willing to make the first move.

Need more convincing? Bars are loud, so you often find yourself shouting yourself hoarse and having to pretend you can hear what the other person is saying when you're really only catching every third word. It's a shame when you meet for dinner the next week and find out that what you thought he was saying about helping to fund the arts, was actually that he served time for robbing three Kmarts.

We've all been victims of the Sourpuss Friend Syndrome. You know the scenario. You start talking to a woman and her friend is at the bar with the sourpuss face, stirring her drink, looking around, and not having any fun. Finally, just as you're starting to make some progress, she gives a tug on your girl's shirt and barks, "Let's get out of here." It gives me chills just thinking about it. Why compete? If you were to meet that same woman the next afternoon at the supermarket while she was alone, your chances of making contact and ending up on a date with her skyrocket.

Simply put, bars are unnatural places to meet people to date. Our daily routines are natural. They're our lives. At night, in a bar, we put on our hottest outfits and we have too many expectations of what our night should be. Our defenses are up and there is too much competition. If you want a one-night stand, I say go to a bar and roll the dice. If you want to meet people to date instead, there are better places to find them.

places to meet people within your daily routine

When I talk to frustrated singles, one of the things that concerns me most is the fear that so many of them have of meeting people on their own. When we were young, small, and helpless, it made sense for our mothers to warn us about talking to strangers. Yet, now that we're fully grown and old enough to have acquired a little bit of good judgment, we should, in principle, be more open-minded.

Think about this: You chose the place you live. While there were probably many factors that went into that decision, one of them is that your area was likely filled with people like you. People who were attracted by the same things that attracted you to that place, like the culture, the landscape, the prevalent industries, even the kinds of restaurants and stores that line the streets of the neighborhood.

Still, our natural tendency is to avoid the people who surround us. We're more willing to give our phone number to a drunk we've met at a bar than we are to say hello to the person who's searching the same aisles at the local supermarket or sitting beside us on the bus. Somewhere in the backs of our minds is that age-old fear that strangers are bad.

Hopefully, the following list of places we all visit as part of our daily routines will help you look at them, and the people you meet there, more optimistically. Our goal is to take a proactive approach with these places. I'll even include pointers about the best times to visit and how to use these environments to deduce relevant pieces of information about your fellow patrons. After you've read about them and see why I like them, you can use your own common sense and intuition to connect the dots and figure out other places that are good meeting spots.

One other thing to keep in mind: Because these are places you frequent regularly, there's a chance that you'll run into the same people time after time. This is what I call the Repeat Factor. Familiarity, in this case, is a good thing. When you can recognize someone, the negative connotations usually associated with strangers vanish, and it's much easier to have a natural conversation.

COFFEE SHOPS

People don't subject themselves to the slow service from the person in the green smock for nothing. The fact is, they can stay at home and drink cheaper coffee. Whether consciously or sub-consciously, people who choose to go to coffee shops go to be social and would often like to meet someone, or, at the very least, would be open to a nice conversation. Coffee shops are what bars used to be except without all the drunken idiots. Instead of the inebriated Drips and Droolers, you're dealing with the overly caffeinated. Believe me, they're much more conducive to conversation and there's a better chance they'll remember it.

Several years ago in Los Angeles, I became an almost permanent fixture at a local coffee shop. I was the Host and if a conversation wasn't in progress, I initiated one. I talked to everyone, was friendly and inviting, and within a couple of months, had an amazing network of friends and acquaintances.

On Saturdays and Sundays we'd all meet up, sit outside from morning until early evening, and talk about dating, sex (or lack thereof), politics, and the entertainment industry. Everyone around us wanted to join our little group because people like to belong. They wanted to be in the middle of the action. We were stimulating, interesting, and welcoming. No one was left out. As a result, all of our dating lives improved dramatically.

I've always found coffee shops to be some of the best places for starting up conversations. Maybe you're not the Host type, maybe you're just a Sitter. Either way, the next time you go sit at the coffee shop, sit next to another solitary Sitter and strike up a conversation. Talk to them about the latest overpriced block-buster in the movie theater or the slanted bias they're reading in the newspaper. Don't worry about bothering them until they give you a clear sign that you are.

Best Times: Weekday mornings before 10:00, weekday evenings after 7:00, all day on weekends. In certain cities, at nights and on weekends, coffee shops are hubs for young professionals to sit back, relax, drink a cup of coffee, or even nap.

Repeat Factor: It depends on your neighborhood. If it looks like a coffee shop that has repeat clientele, it probably is. However, there's no guarantee. You may see someone there a hundred times or never again. Check to see how friendly they are with the staff and the other customers. This can be a good indicator of how often they come.

Added Benefits: You can become friendly with the employees even if you're not too fond of their service. This is Flirt Practice and you're becoming the Safe Person by having pre-established relationships within the environment. An added benefit to getting to know patrons of the coffee shop is you'll get to know their friends, and being introduced through others can make things a whole lot easier.

THE SUPERMARKET

The supermarket has a relaxed atmosphere where people usually take their time finding items to buy. It's always easier to start a conversation with someone who's lingering. You can simply walk up to somebody and introduce yourself, or you can find a creative way into conversation. Use the environment. Pay attention to what they have in their baskets or what they're looking at on the shelf. Start a conversation about Frosted

Flakes. It really doesn't make a difference, as long as you're talking. The majority of people will be receptive and you'll most likely get into a nice discussion.

Make friends with the people who work in the supermarket. Talk to the guy at the deli counter or the lady at the cash register. Get to know them. Why? Not only is it important to be friendly to as many people as possible, but it'll make you seem that much more safe once you start talking to someone you're interested in if all your supermarket employee friends give you a warm reception. You'll come off as friendly, likeable, and familiar.

For instance, say you're about to check out and you see someone you're attracted to in another line. You go and change lines and get behind the person. Instead of looking at the floor or ceiling like you usually would, you notice that Cathy is the cashier. Because you know Cathy, you say hello, and strike up a conversation with her. Immediately, the person in front of you will turn around to see with whom Cathy is speaking. It's human nature. There's your moment to strike up a conversation with the person in whom you're interested.

Best Times: Weekdays between 6:00 and 8:00 P.M. On Sundays, between 4:00 and 7:00 P.M. Two to four hours before special events like the Super Bowl or the Oscars and any day before, or the morning of, a major holiday.

Repeat Factor: Pretty good. People are creatures of habit. They do the same things repeatedly, like hamsters on a wheel, especially when it comes to necessities like buying food.

Added Benefits: If you shop in a place with a café, then you may be able to have an instant first date. Also, by observing the contents in a person's cart, you may get some idea of whether or not they're single. If they're really loading up, then it's possible that they're living with someone. This doesn't mean you should automatically assume it's a member of the opposite sex. It may be a roommate, a friend in town, or they may be doing a favor for a sick neighbor. Just be aware. If you see a woman purchasing four steaks, men's underarm deodorant, and loads of beer, then there's a strong probability that she may be living with a man in a romantic sense. But you'll never know until you start talking.

BOOKSTORES

When you bought this book, did you take notice of how many people were in your local bookstore? If you go to the bookstore at the right time, you will find dozens of singles buying books, sitting in the aisles reading, and browsing. Once again, people linger for a reason. They can read at home. They don't need to sit in a bookstore, they choose to. In addition, because bookstores such as Barnes & Noble have combined forces with Starbucks and are taking over the world, people are taking books and magazines into the coffee shop and reading there.

Pay careful attention to what others are reading and browsing through. It's extremely easy to tell someone you have read the book they're looking at and either recommend it or not. Again, observe. The more you observe, the more you will have to talk about. Ask someone if they can recommend a book to you. Look out for signs. If someone is slyly looking over your shoulder at what book you're holding in your hands, it might be an open invitation to a conversation. Once you're discussing the book, the conversation can go anywhere. The two of you may even wind up joining each other in the coffee shop for a double latte frappuccino.

Best Times: Weeknights between 7:00 and 9:00 P.M. and even later if it's a bookstore with a coffee shop. On the weekends, bookstores are busy all day long and even at night. Every time I've gone to the bookstore on a Friday or Saturday night, I've found dozens of singles reading and studying. Like you, sometimes people don't want to go out on the town; they prefer a cozy evening surrounded by information and literature. If you take advantage of the opportunity, you could end up spending it with them, which in turn could lead to a date on a different day.

Repeat Factor: Lousy. If you see someone you'd like to talk to, be proactive and go after them.

Added Benefit: You'll be around books and periodicals. Take this time to read, brush up on the hot new authors, or get reacquainted with the classics. Education is the key to success in the working world and it's very attractive to members of the opposite sex. By spending time in a bookstore, you'll always have more things to talk about.

MOVIE THEATERS

The movie theater is yet another place where people usually don't think about meeting other singles. Why? Are couples the only people who go to see movies while all the singles sit home or get drunk in a bar? Of course not. Everyone goes to the movies. The next time you're there, look around for single people by themselves or with their friends and get behind them in line for popcorn, the ticket line, or sit behind them in the theater.

Look in the newspaper to get an idea of what's playing. If you're a woman, go check out the latest action film. Chances are there will be many single men bonding by watching Vin Diesel or Bruce Willis kick some celluloid butt. If you're a man, go look for the latest light romantic comedy. Surely, there will be some ladies in there to see Jennifer Lopez fall in love for the thirteenth unrealistic time. (Kind of mirrors her real life, doesn't it?)

Granted, it's a slight generalization that men watch action and women watch romantic comedy. However, there's a reason for the stereotype. If you want to get more specific, you can go past genre. If you love an auteur such as Woody Allen or Martin Scorsese, then you shouldn't be surprised to find others who love them as well.

The first thing I think about when I go to a less mainstream movie is how cool it is that there are actually so many people interested in the same thing or, at the very least, curious to see what that film or filmmaker is all about. Unfortunately, after the movie is over no one talks about it, even though we're all usually bursting to. Ask yourself a question: When you're shuffling out of the movie theater like sheep, why not turn to the stranger next to you and ask them what they thought of the movie? It's that easy.

Best Times: Weekdays between 7:00 and 9:00 P.M. On rainy weekends in the summer, and even Friday or Saturday nights are a great time.

Repeat Factor: None. This is a one-shot deal.

Added Benefit: You'll keep abreast of new movies, new directors, new actors, and you'll enjoy the already established ones. Moreover, you'll always have something to talk about.

DEPARTMENT STORES AND BOUTIQUES

Virtually all types of stores are easy places to meet new people because they all have the browsing or lingering factor in common. Shopping is an activity. Usually, we're in no rush to leave.

One of the tricks to meeting people while shopping is to branch out of your sex-specific areas. If you're a woman, spend some time in the men's section. Look at the latest styles. See who the hot male designers are. If you see a man trying on some clothing, pick up a shirt that you like and say you think it would look good on him. If you get into a conversation and he asks what you're doing in the men's section, you can tell him that you're gift shopping for a friend.

The same goes for men. Look around the women's department. Ask someone you find attractive if you think that your sister or close female friend would like a pair of pants like the ones you're holding. You can tell them that you were considering buying them as a gift, and could really use a female opinion. You're guaranteed to start a conversation with this tactic, and get some gift-giving advice in the process.

We're all opinionated. You have a great conversation opener in any kind of store simply by asking someone what he or she thinks of the jewelry, CD, furniture, or poster you're contemplating.

Best Times: Weekends year round and ideally in the summer, especially after 3:00 P.M. All day, any day if it's raining or cloudy. Anytime there's a sale that you can usually find advertised in the local paper. The days leading up to (especially the weekend preceding) a major holiday are also great times. Don't limit your Christmas shopping to two hours to get it over with. Spread your shopping out over several days.

Repeat Factor: Not good. Many of these stores are too big, may not be in your neighborhood, and cater to people from all over your city. Act, or you'll probably miss an opportunity.

Added Benefit: You'll keep abreast of all the latest trends in fashion, jewelry, music, etc. It'll help to keep you well-rounded and up with the times—always an attractive quality to members of the opposite sex.

THE GYM

People go to the gym to make themselves feel good. It's also a place where people walk around half naked. You'd have to be practically asexual not to take notice of the people around you at the gym.

Nevertheless, the gym can be a tricky pickup spot. Some men and women don't like to be bothered while working out or while participating in a class. It's important to take it slow, and watch the signs. If you see someone you like working out, an easy conver-sation opener is to simply ask if you can work in sets with them.

Best Times: Weekdays after 5:00 P.M., and late mornings on Saturday and Sunday.

Repeat Factor: As good as it gets. There's no rush to ask someone out at the gym because you'll most likely see them again, possibly three to four times a week. Staying in shape requires consistent effort, so their gym visits are likely to be an integrated part of their routines. Take advantage of this by allowing casual friendships to develop first. This way, after you've gotten to know someone a little bit and they feel comfortable with you, you can ask them out for a drink or coffee.

Added Benefit: Adrenaline is a powerful stimulus, and a toned figure helps give you more confidence, which helps you in all aspects of your social life.

YOGA

As an alternative or addition to the gym, yoga is the new hot form of fitness sweeping over America. Unfortunately for women, and fortunately for men, the ratio is usually 5 to 1 in favor of the guys. Therefore, if you're a man who doesn't mind putting your body through ninety minutes of pure torture in unnatural positions, this is a great place to meet someone.

Keep in mind that yoga is a total mind and body experience, so some people might be too absorbed to welcome a quick approach. When you do talk to someone, make it simple and make it relate to what you're doing. Be patient. If you get involved, you'll see the same people repeatedly. After you've been to class a few times and have made some friendships, then you can ask someone out for a drink, coffee, or even a wheat grass shot (which is a cross between chewing on the lawn and eating dirt).

Best Times: Weekdays after 5:00 P.M. and all day on the weekends.

Repeat Factor: Fantastic! Most people who practice yoga take classes on a regular basis. I do.

Added Benefit: Flexibility. Peace of mind. A community of people who share similar interests.

BEAUTY SALONS

Find a great beauty salon in your city that cuts both men's and women's hair and you may be in for a treat. You should also get to know your hairstylist on a personal level. Stylists get very intimate with their clients and know all about their personal lives. If your stylist likes you and you let them know you're available, they may have another client of theirs to set you up with. Again, another reason to be friendly to everyone you meet.

Best Times: Weekdays after work, mornings, and afternoons on the weekends. Also, New Year's Eve day.

Repeat Factor: Bad, but again, get to know your stylist and the people that work there. You never know who they may want to introduce you to.

Added Benefit: You'll be looking your best! Also, there's a waiting area. Always scan the waiting area to see who you can strike up a conversation with.

LIBRARIES

Playboy magazine once put out a list of the best pickup spots in the country. University libraries made the list. Remember, not everyone studying in a university library is in college. Some are in medical school, law school, and getting other higher level degrees. People of all ages go back to school. Even if you're fifty, this a good place to check out.

Unfortunately, if you're not a student, university libraries can be strict about who can get in. If you're not a student, call to see if you can get access. If you can't, you may want to sit outside and read on a nice day. Inevitably, singles will be walking in and out, or reading around the library perimeter.

Public libraries, especially those in big cities or with large reading rooms, can be great places to meet people, too.

Best Times: All day during weekdays and all weekend. Students are constantly studying. The best times at a public library are between 7:00 to 9:00 P.M. weekdays, and all day on the weekends.

Repeat Factor: Favorable and unfavorable. If you're a student, the Repeat Factor is much better than if you're a visitor, because many people go to the library and sit in the same spot as part of their daily routine and you'll inevitably run into them again.

Added Benefit: Again, like in the bookstore, books and information surround you. Take advantage. Learn something new.

AIRPORTS AND AIRPLANES

All day, every day, singles are traveling, sometimes for business, sometimes for pleasure. Travelers often wind up spending significant amounts of downtime in the airport, sitting near their gates, or in the bars and restaurants in the terminal. Bars in airports are different from other types of bars; they're much more relaxed and casual. In the current traveling climate, people often spend so much time in the airport that they'd likely love the monotony to be interrupted by some friendly conversation.

It gets a little bit trickier when you actually board the plane. If you see someone attractive and no one is sitting next to them, wait until the plane has finished boarding, and then ask the stewardess if you can move to a more comfortable seat. Usually, they'll say yes. It really doesn't matter why you move as long as there's an open seat next to someone you're interested in. However, take caution. There's nothing worse than being stuck next to an Altitude Talker, and you don't want to become one yourself. It can be tempting to mistake the captivity of your audience for genuine interest. Pay attention to the signs. If they hand you a sleeping pill or rent you a headset for the movie, they're probably not interested. If all goes well, you will have a natural opportunity at the end of the flight to ask for a number.

The trick, in both of these scenarios, is finding someone who lives in your area. This is not to say that you couldn't go out with someone in another town, it just makes it more difficult. I happened to have a client who lived in New York and met a woman on an airplane from Miami who was heading north to visit friends. When she went back to Miami, they kept in touch and eventually began visiting each other. Today, they're married with two children.

Best Times: Anytime you fly.

Repeat Factor: None, unless you like hanging out in airports.

Added Benefit: Frequent-flyer miles.

DRY CLEANERS

Surprised? You shouldn't be. We all have clothes that we dry clean occasionally, and most people find one dry cleaner either close to home or close to work. Check out your area and see which cleaners happen to have the most people you're attracted to walking in and out. Then go down there and get on line.

Because it's not the type of place we linger in, meeting someone at the dry cleaners is a slightly more difficult encounter. If you're helped first, fight the urge to leave as soon as you're finished. Stick around and continue the conversation while the dry cleaner is going through their things, or wait outside the store, where you can then walk with them, talk some more, and close the deal.

Best Times: After work Monday through Friday and Saturday, late morning, before lunch.

Repeat Factor: Weak. People go in and out so quickly it's hard to catch them at the precise time they're there. If you see someone, you have to act quickly.

Added Benefit: Your clothes are clean, which is always attractive to the opposite sex. Also, if you see someone you're interested in, check out what they're getting cleaned. You may be able to get an idea if they're single or not. Women, if a man's carrying a dress, he's either a cross-dresser or there's a good possibility he's living with someone. Men, if a woman is carrying a man's suit, she's either into the androgynous look or may be living with a man.

THE GAS STATION

The gas station is a good place to meet people because there's nothing to do when you're filling up your car with gas. Most of us spend this time staring off into space, looking at the road, or taking in our surroundings, but it doesn't have to be that way.

Next time you are at the gas station, take a look around to see who is filling up around you. Instead of daydreaming, start up a conversation with someone. Some effective and easy topics: Talk about how much you like their car or how high the price of gasoline has become.

Best Times: Weekday mornings before work. Weekday evenings after work. All daytime hours on the weekend.

Repeat Factor: Zip! People are in and out quickly and there's usually no routine as to when people fill up their car.

Added Benefit: Since filling up your car is as expensive as a good meal out, at least now you have the opportunity to get a phone number out of it.

WORK

A client of mine, Jason, was sitting on the phone one day at work speaking to a woman at another corporation. They had never met face to face, but they spoke frequently and he found her voice and words warm, inviting, and friendly. He started daydreaming about what she looked like. After they'd finished discussing work that day, my client carefully and skillfully took the conversation from a professional level, to a personal one. He began by asking her simple questions about where she was originally from, where she had gone to college, and how she liked her job. Take note: People love to talk about themselves.

One thing led to another, and they agreed to meet for drinks. Risky, you might say. How many times have you thought about the person behind the voice, but rationalized inaction? Well, because my client listened to me, and took the risk of meeting someone he'd never seen before, he's presently married to the very same woman.

Now, Jason could have gotten himself into a lot of trouble. Unfortunately, one of the backlashes of attempting personal conversation in a workplace is that it can be interpreted or perceived as sexual harassment. Still, everyday, people are meeting people through work, and ending up in relationships. Statistics also show that after school work is one of the most likely places to meet a mate.

Asking someone out who you work with directly on a daily basis can be a bad idea unless you want to be the topic of conversation at the watercooler—or worse, standing in front of a judge for inappropriate conduct. However, if you do want to spend more time with someone, find out what they do on the weekends and then invite them and their friends to meet you and some of your friends. That way it's innocent and you'll get to know them outside the work environment. Then, you'll see if they're as attracted to you as you are to them. If they're not, drop it immediately and when you see them again, ask them about some of their friends. Start Network Dating.

Best Times: When a safe opportunity presents itself. Furthermore, many industries have conventions, networking events, and parties. Utilize these to help build your network.

Repeat Factor: If you work with them, then you see them everyday. Develop friendships. Go to lunches. Then take it to the next level when you have some indication that they'll be receptive.

Added Benefit: The environment naturally lends itself to two people having things in common. Shared work or experiences, and similar goals.

places you can go outside of your daily routine

There are tons of places to go to outside of your daily routine. Below I've listed just a few. After reading these, you should be able to come up with some of your own. Try to think outside the box. Always ask yourself, Where, on a particular day or at a particular time of year, would you be most likely to meet another single?

PARTIES AND WEDDINGS

There are many different types of parties you can attend. Birthday parties, housewarming parties, dinner parties, office parties, engagement parties, holiday parties, retirement parties, wedding parties, confirmation parties, and Bar Mitzvah parties. Actually, the reasons why someone would have a party are endless. I've even been to an "I just got fired" party.

We're all invited to parties once in a while and we should all take advantage of a party as a place to meet new people. In fact, you can even host your own parties and use them as a guise to improve your dating life. Throw an "I'm miserable that I'm single" dinner party occasionally, invite your friends, and tell each friend to bring a guest you've never met before who's single. Have a birthday party for yourself at a restaurant, send out an e-mail, and tell everyone you know to bring anyone they want. The more the merrier.

All of these situations can provide you with endless potential dates. If you're at a party thrown by someone else, use the host. Have them introduce you to someone you're interested in. Once you start talking with that person, ask them how they know the host.

Take note: Weddings are one of the best places to meet other singles because The Vulnerability Factor is at an all time high. When your friend is planning the wedding, tell them to make sure you are at the table with the most singles. You'll then be face to face with other vulnerable singles wondering when their time will come. Carpe Wedding Diem!

Best Times: Whenever they are thrown or you want to throw one.

Repeat Factor: Within a social circle you might have some friends in common, so you may see them again, but don't count on it. It may be a long time. I recommend acting immediately in these situations.

Added Benefit: You get to socialize with old friends and make new ones. Expanding your social circle is always a major plus, even if it's with people of your sex. You never know who they may know and what invitations you may get to other parties. Again, network dating.

HIKING TRAILS/BIKE PATHS/PARKS

If you love the great outdoors, you're not alone. During the warmer parts of the year people seek outdoor activities. In areas with warm climates, people seek them out year 'round. Many cities, like Los Angeles, have dozens of hiking trails, bike paths, and parks to go to. Most cities, at the very least, have parks.

The outdoors is a great place to meet people because it's extremely relaxing. On nice days, parks are full of people who go there to read, catch some sun, or play sports. If you've ever seen Central Park's Great Lawn when it gets warm outside, then you know what I'm talking about. It's a singles paradise.

If you go to a park, take a blanket or towel with you, find

someone who's attractive, and sprawl out near them. Be aware of them. You will know soon enough if they're receptive or not.

Best Times: Early evenings and weekends. It goes without saying that the best times of year to be in parks or on hiking trails are in the spring, summer, and fall. But don't rule out the winter months: Lots of people like to take walks alone to clear their heads or look at how beautiful and clean the snow is.

Repeat Factor: Almost nonexistent.

Added Benefit: Getting in touch with nature. Exercise. Time to clear your head and relax.

THE DOG PARK

Dog parks are quite possibly the easiest place to meet other singles. They're relaxed, nonthreatening environments, and everyone there already has something in common—a love of dogs. If you go regularly, you'll quickly become a member of a canine-loving community full, at least in part, of other singles who have dogs for companionship. Look out for people who seem to be having a good time with their dogs, and may be receptive to a conversation.

Best Times: In the evenings when owners take their dogs out themselves, and all day on the weekends.

Repeat Factor: Pretty good. If you go to the dog park at the same time every day, or even every weekend, you'll most likely run into the same people repeatedly.

Added Benefit: Being around animals. Being outside. Being around other people who love dogs. It's great for your dog, too.

ORGANIZATIONS/POLITICAL CAMPAIGNS

There are a million different organizations with which you can become involved. You know what you're interested in. What's great about joining a social action group is that you'll meet people who share a common interest with you. Also, it'll make you feel good about yourself that you're giving back and getting involved.

Try volunteering for a political campaign as well. There are thousands of committed citizens, many of them single, who are very passionate about politics. If there are no singles in your office, develop a relationship with someone there, and let them know that you're willing to be set up with their single friends.

Best Times: Whenever the meetings are scheduled. Year 'round for organizations and during election years for campaigns.

Repeat Factor: Very good. Some people may just be trying it out, but most people who get involved stay involved.

Added Benefit: Giving back to the world. Expanding your horizons. Learning more about the political system, a candidate, how government works, and what goes on in the world.

VACATIONS

Earlier, I talked about the Vacation Mentality. Once we're out of our everyday environments, we become more relaxed and open to experience, and we should strive to incorporate those attitudes into our lives at home. But what makes vacations particularly great opportunities is that they're one of the only places lots of singles go for the specific purpose of trying to meet people.

Look online or call a travel agent and tell them you're single and you want to go to a destination frequented by other singles or even on a cruise. If you don't have a friend or family member to go with, consider going alone. It may be daunting at first, but you'll be that much more motivated to reach out to new people. I've had several clients who've taken off for a week trip by themselves only to return with a girlfriend or boyfriend. Take small trips too—you don't always need a week to go somewhere. If you live in New York, take a drive up the New England coast for the weekend. If you live in Los Angeles, head up to Santa Barbara. If you live in Iowa, check out Nebraska. If you want to take a walk on the wild side, go south to New Orleans. One of the greatest tour operators for singles, ages 18 to 35, is Contiki Tours. Although I've never been on a Contiki Tour myself, I've had numerous clients and friends experience it, and every one of them raved about what a great time they had.

Best Times: As often as possible.

Repeat Factor: None.

Added Benefit: You're not working!

I'll conclude this chapter with one of my favorite examples of how easy it is to meet people anytime and anywhere. To people who have traditionally not been good at meeting new people, taking a taxi and getting a date seem outrageous. How often do we even agree to share with a stranger? Well, maybe this story will soften you up.

TAXIS

Several years ago, I was in New York. It was a cold night and I was standing on the corner for a long time waiting for a taxi to pass by. After a few minutes, an attractive woman walked up next to me. She didn't put her hand up in the air to wave for a taxi because she knew I'd been there first. As I waited, my cell phone rang, and it was a woman I had been set up on a blind date with that night. While the blind date was nice, at that moment I really couldn't take my eyes off the woman standing next to me on the corner.

In a moment of inspiration, I turned to her and acted as if the woman on the other line was just yapping my ear off. With my hand, I simulated a mouth. The woman on the corner started to laugh and after I hung up the phone, she asked me if it was my girlfriend with whom I'd been speaking. I confessed to her that it was not a girlfriend, but a blind date, at which point we got into a whole conversation about blind dating in New York. We even relayed a few of our own stories.

By the time a cab finally arrived, we'd figured out that we were both going downtown and agreed to split it. Five minutes later, the cab stopped at her street. As she was handing me money to split the fare, I told her that I'd had a great time talking to her, and would love to continue our conversation. She gave me her number, and we dated several times. So you can see: There are no rules. If you remain an open and friendly person, opportunities like this will fall into your lap.

Best Times: Weekend nights in big cities. The taxi line in big city airports can also be a good opportunity anytime. Get on a taxi line and see if someone you're interested in wants to split a cab with you.

Repeat Factor: Zero, unless you drive a taxi for a living.

Added Benefits: Even if you don't get a date, you split half the taxi fare and save some money. If your companion is a gentleman, you might even get a free ride.

making contact

Until now, I've covered the mind-set you need to achieve to meet new people, the personal grooming and fashion to help you look your best when meeting new people, and when and where to meet single people like yourselves. Now, as promised earlier, I'm going to teach you what to do and say when you zone in on a person who interests you.

In this section, the interpersonal communication skills I teach apply mainly to meeting people about town and build upon the last part you read. However, in this section, there are also a few pointers you can use when venturing into the blind dating and Internet dating worlds. Remember, always use all three forms of meeting new people to date—blind dating, Internet dating, and meeting people about town.

You will find that this section is broken up into eight chapters. The first four solely apply to meeting people about town. The second four also apply to meeting people about town and also have bits and pieces of information that you can and should incorporate into your approach when blind dating and Internet dating. Some of these bits and pieces directly relate to communicating with another person, and some of them are philosophical outlooks you should further incorporate into your dating mindset.

By the time you're done reading this section of the book, you will have at your disposal all of the tools you'll need to master the dating process. From then on, it's up to you to implement what I've taught, and to use it in a positive and productive way. If it helps, take notes when reading this section and try to imagine yourself in the various scenarios I present. Visualization is the first step to incorporation. Visualize and you will start to realize. Realize, and you'll never kick yourself again for letting that cute girl or guy get away.

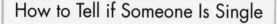

· 6 ·

How to Tell if Someone Is Single

In the previous section, Meeting People About Town, I hinted at some ways to tell if someone you desire is available. I recommend that you not spend too much of your time pondering whether or not someone is single and open to being approached. The last thing I want either my clients or my readers to do is stall, psyche themselves out, and miss the pickup. If the person you're fixated on is unavailable, you'll find out soon enough. Yet, you'll do it the gutsy way—by approaching them and starting a conversation. The cowardly way is to make an assumption and never make an approach.

Most of the time, unless someone is wearing a ring, holding hands with someone of the opposite sex, or kissing someone in front of you, you simply won't know the answer until you strike up a discussion with them. However, because I'm asked this question so often by so many clients, here are some signs you can interpret.

clear signs someone is not single ·······················

The most obvious clear sign that someone isn't single is that they're wearing a wedding ring. Several years ago, I knew a guy who loved the challenge of breaking up marriages. Nine out of ten times when going after a woman, he'd hunt down women with husbands. Eventually, we nicknamed him "The Lord of the Rings"—wedding rings, that is. Unfortunately, he was a nightmare for husbands—handsome, suave, and debonair—he often succeeded in his home-wrecking quests. What was his infatuation with married women? Was it the challenge of trying to attain a committed woman? Probably. And this much I know—he's not alone.

For a multitude of reasons, married people are attractive to us. In fact, many times they're more attractive to us married than they were single. For example, I once had a then recently married ex-client who called me one day laughing hysterically. "David," he said. "How come when I was single women never approached me and now that I have that big gold wedding band on my finger I get hit on all the time?"

After much pondering, the only answer I could come up with is that people are attracted to what the wedding ring symbolizes—specifically maturity, commitment, loyalty, dedication, stability, strength, and confidence. Most importantly, it says that someone is taken—paradoxically one of the sexiest qualities a person can possess. People love what they can't have.

In addition, that little alloy around a finger permanently erases the flashing desperation sign on our foreheads—you know, the one that haunts us when we're single. The ironic part is that once people reach this level of commitment that represents so many attractive qualities we admire, we can no longer have them—well, at least in theory.

While the statistics are at times unfavorable for married couples, it doesn't mean that you need to be the catalyst to begin their ruin. You don't need to be the Mt. Vesuvius that erupts onto their marriage. I'm not being judgmental about people who have affairs, I'm just being practical as your advisor on the dating scene. It's my job to inform you that there are plenty of great single people out there to date and there's no need for you to go sticking your fingers in the cookie jar. A tremendous amount of baggage comes with getting involved with a married person. Most of the time these so-called affairs never lead anywhere except to the unmarried person feeling heartbroken and used. Trust me, your hours are much more constructively spent pursuing available people.

This advice particularly applies to women. Statistics show that up to 70 percent of men cheat on their wives, and let me be the first to inform you that they aren't cheating with their Border collie—they're cheating with you.

"But David," one of my clients once said to me. "He just looked so cute in his white T-shirt and jeans and playing with his children, that I just melted right then and there. I couldn't help myself." Now, I'll tell you the same thing I told my former client: "Spare me." If you want to see the soft side of a man, make a date with a single guy, take him back to your place, and show him *Old Yeller*. Stay away from Mr. Fruit of the Loom and his children. Your time is much better served with a single man.

There are other obvious signs that a person is involved with someone else. For instance, if you're standing on the street corner and you see two people lip-locked and the woman is holding roses in one hand and has her other hand on his butt, you can bet that she isn't available for a pickup. Don't bother even looking—keep moving on. I guarantee you that within a one-block radius there are probably five or six great single prospects.

not-so-clear signs someone is single

Occasionally, we all happen onto those moments when we're actually unclear if someone is involved or not. There's no dead giveaway like a wedding ring or face sucking on a street corner to give us an indication. We've all at one time or another been sitting at a coffee shop, seen an attractive man or woman sitting with someone of the opposite sex, and wondered if they were friends, family, or lovers.

In an event such as this, take notice of how the two people are interacting with one another. Are they touching each other? Are they affectionate? How close are they sitting? How close are they walking? Are they holding hands? If you sense that after asking yourself these questions that the two people are involved in an intimate physical relationship, move on. Again, there are many others out there. However, if you have a strong feeling the two people aren't involved and you see an opportunity to approach the person, don't let the moment pass you by. That cute guy or girl may just be taking their little sister or brother out to lunch.

If you're confused, there are subtle ways to find out the answer to your question. For instance, let's say you're a woman and you see another attractive woman walking into a store with an attractive man, and you aren't sure if they're in fact together or not. If not, you'd really like to meet him. The simple solution is to wait for a moment when the man is briefly alone, position yourself near him while you both nonchalantly look through white T-shirts, and say, "Hello." Then, after he says "Hello" back, say, "So, you here shopping with your girlfriend?" If it's not his girlfriend, he'll tell you. The same goes for a man. Just ask in a cool, nonchalant, confident, and playful way, and you'll get your answer.

clearest signs someone is single

Although not foolproof, there are certain signs that indicate someone's single. The most obvious sign is if you get approached for a pickup. Granted, that person may already be in a relationship, or just looking to make a new friend, but most of the time it's safe—they're looking to meet you. If someone approaches you and begins to talk, play it out as if you're sure they're single.

Another sign someone's single is when someone approaches you and simply makes small talk. As I'll teach you later in this section, there are several different methods for making contact with strangers. Small talk is one of the many indirect ways for someone to make contact with you. The exchange can be about anything— a pen you're holding, a book you're reading, a newspaper under your arm, your coat, your shoes, your watch—anything at all. Take notice of these moments and seize upon them. Don't stand there with your head in the clouds. Pick up on the fact that someone is making contact with you—and usually it's for a good reason—they're interested. I specifically emphasize this with women who all too often get approached and think nothing of it. If someone approaches you and asks to borrow a pen, start talking to him. He could have gone and asked anybody to use their pen—but he chose you. Get it?

You also need to pay attention to body language. Throughout this book, I've harped on you about becoming more aware. This is where those skills particularly come into play. Chances are that if that guy across the room is looking in your direction, he's not looking at the clock over your head. Men are bad at hiding their interest in a woman they find attractive. We tend to stare intently at what we find desirable. Pick up on the signal. If you find him attractive, don't wait for him to disappear, and if he's not making a move—you make it first. Notice things like people smiling at you. It's almost a surefire way to tell if someone is single. Think about it—smiling is not a natural facial expression. We have to move a lot of muscles in our faces to produce a single smile. That means someone is making an effort. Smile back. Open your mouth and say the magic word, "Hello."

I'm sure there have been many times that you've observed someone within a social setting looking around aimlessly. This is usually another tell-tale sign that someone's single. They may be out with friends or alone in a crowded place, but chances are, they're probably looking for someone else, as opposed to being bored with their atmosphere. One last way to tell if someone's single is when they're out by themselves or with friends of the same sex on a Saturday or Sunday morning. If so, chances are they're available and there's no significant other who spent the night and woke up to join them that morning for a stroll or brunch.

· 7 ·

Getting Over Anxiety

In Your Mental Makeover, I first discussed anxiety. As promised, I'll touch on the topic again, because in the next several parts of the book I'll be teaching you how to approach a person you find desirable. However, before you can approach someone, you must first learn how to relax. The question is, what makes us so nervous? Here's my theory:

From the first moment we lay eyes on others we find attractive, we put them into what I call a Fantasy Box. We begin to fantasize about the person and imagine ourselves being with them. We wonder what they're like, and then make assumptions about them. While all this is going on, we're simultaneously psyching ourselves out of ever approaching them. Most of the time we don't mean to—it just happens—and by the time we're done thinking about the person, we've put them on such a pedestal that we hesitate and never do anything about it.

Hesitation can be deadly in the meeting game. The longer you fantasize and the longer you wait to make an approach, the more anxiety overcomes you, and you wind up doing nothing. Anxiety produces what I call Monkey Chatter—voices in your head that discourage you from taking action. Your stomach tightens, a lump forms in your throat, and sometimes you even break into a cold sweat. Suddenly, your mind starts circulating excuses as to why you shouldn't approach the person. "He's too good looking, he's out of my league." "It's not the right time or place." "If she wanted to talk to me, she'd approach me." "I look fat in these jeans." "My hair doesn't look good." "He's probably gay." Sound familiar?

The variety of excuses that fill your head are infinite and what fills one's head varies from person to person. We all have our own personal demons to contend with. Yet, as infinite as the demons can be, the same remedy exists for them all—to act before you let the anxiety kick in. In essence, the best way to combat anxiety is to never let it start. Think about it. If you were to parachute out of a plane for the first time, do you think it would be easier to just jump, or to spend five minutes looking 10,000 feet down and contemplating the millions of variables that could lead to your untimely demise? When it comes to meeting new people, the answer is obvious—jump. Earlier in the book, I introduced the Three-Second Principle. Here's where it comes into play:

If you see someone you find attractive and want to meet, approach them within three seconds. Don't hesitate because then you'll have to contend with the Monkey Chatter. If you've just bought a coffee at Starbucks and you spot a cute guy or girl by the condiment table, act, don't wait. You've got three seconds to say hello. The more clever you try to make it, the more it'll seemed forced. Just act.

Granted, acting within three seconds isn't always practical. For example, you could spot someone across the room who's in a conversation and have to wait until they're finished before you approach. In the event this happens and as a result, the Monkey Chatter starts in your brain, I want you to take a deep breath, relax yourself, and run through the following five questions in your head:

1. If I approach this person and they aren't interested, will I die?

2. If I approach this person and they aren't interested, will it end up on the front page of *The New York Times*?

3. If I approach this person and they aren't interested, what does it say about me as a person?

4. If I approach this person and they aren't interested, will it affect the love of my family and friends?

5. If I approach this person and they aren't interested, will it affect my career?

These questions are designed to bring you back out of Monkey Chatter world, re-center you, and deconstruct what you've built up in your head to be the most significant event in both your life and the world. It's not. You won't die, your picture won't be published, if you get rejected it says nothing about you as a person, your family and friends will still love you, and you aren't going to lose your job—unless of course you're asking out the boss's daughter.

Earlier in the book, I talked about the difference between Real Fear and Fake Fear. Remind yourself that this is Fake Fear at work and it's up to you to suppress it. Remind yourself that if you approach this person and they're not interested in getting to know you better, that you'll go on and the whole experience will fade from your memory in a short amount of time. Approaching someone new has absolutely no negative consequences. It only has a potentially positive outcome. Your worst-case scenario in approaching someone is that they don't want to get to know you better. Your best-case scenario is that someone will want to get to know you better and you'll get a date—even better—you may add a special someone to your life. Sounds like pretty good odds, doesn't it?

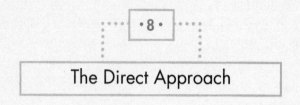

The Direct Approach

We've now covered everything you need to know in preparation for your approach. At this point, you should be feeling confident and ready to take on the simple challenge of meeting someone new. Now, I'll go over how exactly to make the advance. Sometimes these situations can be tricky, sometimes they're very easy. I'll go through as many scenarios as I can to give you an idea of how a successful approach works. Once you begin to employ your own common sense with the techniques and insight I will provide, making contact with a new person should never again be a daunting task.

We're going to go over two main categories of approach: The Direct Approach, to which this chapter is dedicated, and The Indirect Approach, which I will cover in the next chapter. Both approaches are excellent and should be utilized. If one isn't practical for the situation at hand, use the other. As you get better, you'll begin to feel comfortable with using both. Remember the old adage, practice makes perfect.

The Direct Approach is exactly what it sounds like. It's a confident approach without the use of tricks, and will lay it on the line. Remember, pickup lines don't work! They're not as clever as they seem in a moment of desperation and scream artificiality where we should be trying to seem real. However, walking straight up to someone and introducing oneself is something we all find attractive.

We've all heard cheesy pickup lines. "Do you come here often?" "How 'bout those Yankees?" "Do you believe in love at first sight? If not, maybe I should walk by again." Horrible, right? How much cooler would it be if you're a man, to walk up to a woman and say, "Hi. My name is Tom. I was sitting over there and couldn't help noticing how beautiful you were. I had to come over and meet you." Assuming you don't smell like a cesspool, I can't think of many women who wouldn't be flattered to hear such words.

What about if you're a woman and you're at a party? Let's say you're standing and talking with some colleagues from work and across the room a handsome man is holding his martini, speaking with someone. At first chance, you excuse yourself from your conversation, walk straight across the room, and say, "Hi. My name is Annette. I was over there talking with some friends and the second you walked into the room, I zoned out. You have an amazing presence. What's your name?"

Confidence, confidence, confidence. I can't emphasize the importance of confidence enough. For men, this is the difference between the guy who meets a woman one night and goes out with her the next, and the guy who spends his Saturday night on a date with his remote control. For women, this is the difference between the girl who disregards traditional social mores and asks out the guy at the party that she finds attractive, as opposed to being the girl who blends in with the wallpaper. Confidence is the key to success. No doubt you'll encounter that rare moment when your self-assured approach will be rebuffed, but it will almost never be in a humiliating way. Do you really think that the man you approach is going to scream out to the entire party, "Get this psycho away from me!" Of course not. Nine out of ten times, you'll at the very least end up in a stimulating conversation.

What about if you're walking down the street? For some reason, this scenario always produces anxiety in people, as if we feel especially exposed and vulnerable. Or is it perhaps that we think that no one walking down the street wants to be approached because they're on their way somewhere? Granted, there are moments when people *are* in a terrible hurry. In these situations, your awareness and observation skills should clue you in. However, if someone is out taking a casual stroll down the street, why not approach them?

Here's an example: Tony is walking down the street and sees an attractive girl coming at him from the other direction. She doesn't seem to be in a hurry. She's looking around, carrying a backpack, and is obviously headed somewhere—remember, we're all headed somewhere. Just as they're about to pass one another, Tony in a nonstartling way, makes his direct approach.

"Excuse me," Tony says as the woman stops. "My name's Tony. The reason I stopped you is, well, for the last block I was walking I couldn't take my eyes off you. You're very pretty. What's your name?"

"Marissa," the woman says smiling.

"Marissa," Tony repeats. "Where are you headed, Marissa?"

"Oh, I'm just heading down to school," Marissa says. "I'm a law student at NYU."

"That's great," Tony says. "How do you like it?"

"It's hard work," Marissa says. "But I love being back in school."

"I know what you mean," Tony replies. "After college I worked for three years and then went for my MBA. Feels good to jog the brain."

Do you see how easy that is? Do you see how Tony confidently told Marissa the truth? That he had been watching her and found her very attractive. Also, after his introduction, he skillfully used the fact that everyone is going somewhere when they're walking and used it to segue into more conversation. Assuming Marissa is single, Tony should have no problem continuing this conversation and getting Marissa's phone number for a date. As you will continue to see in the scenarios in this book, you don't need to have an hour-long conversation with someone to get their phone number.

The beautiful thing about obtaining dates in the new millennium is the safety of a cellular phone. There was a time before cellular phones that people were reluctant to give out their home phone numbers to people. Women, especially, got nervous that a man they were uninterested in would keep calling them and harassing them to go out on a date. Also, a stalker could use someone's phone number and name to find out where they lived. Today, there's no way to track down where someone lives with just a cell phone number. Your best bet is to ask for their first name and cell phone number during a brief encounter. If they don't want to talk to you after they give you the number, they don't have to. They can just refuse to answer the phone when your number comes up on their caller ID.

The Direct Approach takes guts, but, that shouldn't be a problem for you anymore. You understand that confidence and a straightforward approach are the quickest ways into someone's heart. It's sexy and cool. For those of you who love pop culture, imagine for this one instance that you're a movie star. Muster your self-confidence and cross the room to the person you'd like to meet, smile, use some charm, and say, "Hi. What's your name?"

The Indirect Approach

Have you ever heard about method acting? It's the theory that encourages actors to use objects in the world around them—props—to help them communicate with other characters and with the audience. On stage, a prop can be anything from a coffee cup to a hat. In the real world, the same rule applies: A prop is something that provides support.

A good example of how minimal a prop can be and how much it can help with communication comes from the movie *The Godfather*. In the film, Don Corleone, played by Marlon Brando, sits in a meeting with Virgil Solozzo, discussing the prospect of Corleone's family joining Solozzo in a narcotics venture. Uninterested in the partnership, the Don stands up and pours a drink for Solozzo. Before sitting down to tell him his decision, he reaches down to brush a piece of lint off Solozzo's leg.

That one movement, subtle as it was, was one of the factors that made Brando's performance so brilliant. In that one movement, Brando showed us that his character, a mobster, could also be fatherly, thoughtful, concerned, and friendly—in essence, human. Brando needed to find a way for the Don to connect on a personal level with Solozzo, to show him that even though he was uninterested in the joint venture he appreciated the offer. At that moment, he saw the piece of lint as a prop and it inspired him.

You don't need to give an Academy Award–winning performance to use props for reinforcement or inspiration. If used correctly, the right prop can easily help you segue into a conversation with anyone you want.

Fortunately, the world we live in is a full place, so there's always some type of prop you can use to start a conversation with a stranger. That prop can be something you carry or that is on your person (so that you make yourself more available to be approached), something that another person carries or is on his or her person, or something in the environment. Learning to identify the best props and how to utilize them is the art of The Indirect Approach. It's an easy skill, and one that will only get easier with time and practice. Master this section and you'll never have to search for an icebreaker again.

bringing your own props

How many times have you heard something like, "Nice weather we're having?" As I said in the previous chapter, these pickup lines are notoriously bad conversation starters. They're forced, uncreative, and unproductive. If you're a polite and forgiving person, you might be compelled to respond with an acknowledging, "Mmm hmm," but what you're really thinking to yourself is, "Boring." Right?

One good way to minimize the chance that you'll be stuck fending off feeble advances forever is to make it easier for prospective singles to approach you.

PROP EXAMPLE 1: PETS

If you have a dog, then as far as I'm concerned, you have the best conversation-opener possible. It's right there, wagging its tail, at the end of a leash.

Having a dog attracts people in two ways. First, the urge to pet a cute dog is just too powerful for many people to resist. Second, it tells people on a subconscious level that you're a warm, caring, and nurturing person before they've even talked to you. Once the conversation starts, all you have to do is live up to that impression. Here's a scenario:

One day Jim walks to his favorite coffee shop with his dog, gets some coffee, and sits outside. An attractive woman is walking down the street. She sees them, gets the "Oh my goodness, look at that adorable puppy" look on her face, and makes a beeline for their table.

"She's so cute," the woman says. "Is she a sheepdog?"

"Yes," Jim says. "But not an English sheepdog. She's a French sheepdog. They call them Briards."

"Briards?" the woman says. "I've never heard of that breed."

"I hadn't either, but supposedly they've been around forever," Jim says. "Napoleon used to have about twenty of them running around Versailles."

"What's her name?" the woman asks.

"Sophia," Jim says. "I named her after Sophia Loren."

"I love Sophia Loren," the woman says. "She's so beautiful."

"That's why I named her that," Jim says. "I thought she was so beautiful that it just seemed to fit. I thought about a French name because she's a French dog, but Sophia seemed just right."

"That's sweet," the woman says.

"I'm Jim, by the way," he says.

"I'm Rachel," she replies, feeling increasingly comfortable.

Jim looks down at Rachel petting the dog.

"She likes you," Jim says. "Here, grab a seat."

Rachel sits down.

"So," Jim says. "Do you have a dog?"

Really, it's that easy. The dog takes the pressure off. You no longer have to walk up to someone and start a conversation out of thin air. People approach you, and you already have something in common, even if it's a pretty common something. Jim also made good use of his prop. He has an interesting piece of information about Sophia's breed (which makes him seem thoughtful), he has a good story to tell about her name (which makes him seem cultured and savvy, because he's seen and appreciated classic foreign films), and he projects sensitivity (because he's demonstrated an appreciation for beauty). If Jim is interested in Rachel, he can keep this conversation going on as long as he wants. Not only do they both feel comfortable, but several interesting topics have come out of their short exchange: They can talk about dogs, movies, celebrities, French history, Italian women . . . or anything else that comes to either's mind by association. I like to call these Portal Words—words that serve as an entrance to new conversation and an exit to old conversation.

PROP EXAMPLE 2: BOOKS

We don't all have or want dogs, though, and I'd never advocate getting one for the sole purpose of attracting members of the opposite sex. So let's look at another example of props that are easily accessible and easy to carry around: books. They're small, light, and everybody has some experience with them. One note of caution: Books are not all created equal, so put some thought into what you choose. If you're a man reading *The Idiot's Guide to Hunting Doves,* women probably won't approach you. Similarly, if you're a woman reading a Harlequin romance, not only is it unlikely that the men around you will have read your book, chances are they'll be skeptical about what you're looking for in a mate. Classic and mainstream books are particularly good to carry because other people are more likely to have read them and people love to talk about what they've read.

Recently, *The Da Vinci Code* became a huge bestseller. Everywhere I went people were reading it and talking about the ideas it purported. Look around your bookstore to see what's selling really well. When you're out, don't be afraid to show off the cover so that other people can see what you're reading.

Books are particularly good props because they say something about you, and if someone else loves the same book, then there's a good chance you'll have something in common. For instance, one of my favorite authors is Erica Jong, who wrote the bestseller, *Fear of Flying*. In the United States alone, it sold 7 million copies, and became a hot topic for discussion. If Erica Jong is one of your favorite authors, then by all means, carry *Fear of Flying*. Here's a scenario:

Jill lives in Chicago and works downtown. On her lunch break, she goes across the street to the local deli, orders a sandwich, and sits down. While eating, she opens up a copy of *Fear of Flying* and starts to read. At the table adjacent to her is Steven, who's sitting with two friends. Steven notices Jill's book.

"Great book," Steven says.

Jill looks up at Steven. He's cute and she is immediately impressed that he knows the book she's reading.

"Isn't it great?" Jill says. "This is my third time reading it. I can't believe you've read it."

"Why's that?" Steven asks.

Now Jill has a chance to impress Steven.

"Well, it's basically about a woman's sexual liberation," Jill says. "I didn't think many men were interested in that."

"Of course we are," Steven says. "Men are very interested in women's sexual liberation. It benefits all of us."

Jill laughs.

"To tell you the truth," Steven says. "I probably never would've read it if I hadn't been forced to take a class on feminist literature when I was at Northwestern. I thought I'd hate it, but to this day it's still the only book I've ever read cover to cover in one sitting."

"That's amazing," Jill says. "I went to Northwestern. And I took that class. When did you graduate?"

Easy, right? Jill had something thoughtful to say about the book and Steven found an opportunity to tell her something impressive about himself. Not everyone will have read the book you're reading, but they may ask you about it anyway, and you can still give a considered response. Here, I used *Fear of Flying,* because it has provocative subject matter and makes for good chitchat. You should stick to your own taste. The list of popular authors is endless.

The book, like the dog, is an attention grabber. It draws people to you and says something about you. It gives you the opportunity to show yourself in a positive light.

other people's props

Even if you always travel with your dog, your book, and a wardrobe of clothing baring your college insignia, you should also know how to recognize and use other people's props. Remember: you have to be proactive. Keep on the lookout for the kinds of things we've already talked about, and for other kinds of props you can use yourself. It just may be that the cute guy on the subway reading *The Adventures of Huckleberry Finn* is actively trying to make himself available.

Regardless of intent, there are tons of items that people wear, have, and carry around with them naturally that you can always use. Here's a mixed list of several props that you can find on either a man or woman. All of the following can be used as a way into a conversation: any kind of clothing or accessories—shoes, pants, skirts, blouses, shirts, suits, ties, cuff links, watches, bracelets, rings, earrings, hair clips, scarves, jackets, gloves, hats; and things we carry, like pocketbooks, backpacks, shopping bags, CD players, headphones, cell phones, beepers, makeup, wallets, gum, or even cigarettes.

Starting to get the picture? Every little thing that I mentioned is a conversation just waiting to happen. Don't be intimidated. When in doubt, everybody loves a compliment.

PROP EXAMPLE 3: JEWELRY

Tom pulls into a gas station to fill up his car. After he gets out, he notices Lillian standing at the pump in front of him filling up her Audi. Tom finds her attractive and wants to meet her. He looks closely and notices that she has a pretty bracelet on her wrist. While the gas is pumping, Tom walks over to Lillian.

"Hi," Tom says. "I couldn't help noticing your bracelet. It's really nice. My sister's birthday is coming up and I was trying to think of something different to get her. Would you mind telling me where you got it? By the way, I'm Tom."

Tom shakes her hand.

"Nice to meet you, Tom. I'm Lillian," she says. "Thank you. I got it at this little shop downtown called The Bracelet Factory."

"Do you think they'll have anything like what you're wearing left?" Tom asks.

"Oh yeah," Lillian says. "They have lots of 'em. And in lots of colors too."

"Great," Tom says. "Thanks for the tip. Oh, by the way, how do you like your Audi? I've seen a few on the road and they look really nice."

You can see what Tom did here. He moved away from talking about her bracelet/prop, which two people can only talk about for so long before boredom strikes, to talking about her car/prop. Cleverly, he made a transition to an entirely different topic by being aware of Lillian's things. Tom and Lillian can now talk about cars for a while. That is, at least until somebody starts honking at them to move out of the way.

PROP EXAMPLE 4: MUSIC

Jerry is standing and waiting for the subway in New York. He's listening to his CD player and has his headphones on. Jessica descends the steps and sees Jerry standing there. She looks him over, decides to go for it, and positions herself next to him. Jerry looks over and they give each other nonchalant smiles.

"What are you listening to?" Jessica asks.

Jerry takes off his headphones.

"It's the new Eminem album," Jerry says.

"I love Eminem," Jessica says. "Should I get it?"

"Sure, why not," Jerry says. "He's so controversial and the way he rhymes is insane."

"So true," Jessica says. "Hey! Did you hear that Christina Aguilera challenged him to a wrestling match?"

Again, simple. If Jessica had already had the new Eminem album, they could have talked about specific songs and kept the conversation going for the entire subway ride. If she'd never heard of Eminem, she could have asked about him as an artist, or shared some of her own preferences. However, if she'd never heard of Eminem, she might want to brush up on her pop culture before striking up conversations about music.

props in your surroundings • • • • • • • • • • • • • • • • • • •

The other day I was sitting in my favorite coffee shop reading the newspaper. After a few minutes, I put down the newspaper and decided to really look around at my surroundings. Here's what I saw: Ten to fifteen tables and chairs, a case filled with muffins and bagels, a cash register, and a menu hanging from the ceiling. On the other side of the shop, I saw a short stand with packets of sugar, Equal, and Sweet'N Low, coffee stirs, milk containers, a bottle of honey, and a cinnamon shaker. Behind the counter, I saw bags of ground coffee, a variety of percolators, and an espresso maker. By the door, a newspaper rack that held *The Los Angeles Times,* and above it was a bulletin board for people to post advertisements.

What I've just described is what most people would call the Coffee, Bean, and Tea Leaf on the corner of San Vicente and Barrington in Brentwood, CA. Yet, when most people visit that coffee shop, they only see the picture as a whole. On that day, I saw it in bits and pieces. As I said earlier, you need to start seeing your surroundings as a collection of props. The more acutely aware of the props available all around you wherever you are, the easier it will be for you to start a discussion using one of them. Let's look at a scenario where someone uses a prop within his surroundings.

PROP EXAMPLE 5: MUFFINS

It's a Tuesday morning and Harris is in the coffee shop waiting on line for coffee. Behind Harris is an attractive girl he would love to talk to. Her name is Courtney. Quickly, he checks out his surroundings. He asks himself what he can use for a prop. "Ah," he thinks to himself. "The muffins." Harris is dead on. Muffins are a great and lighthearted conversation opener. Harris bends down to look at the muffins and then looks back up to Courtney.

"They look good don't they?" Harris asks. "Have you ever tried the muffins here?"

"Yes," Courtney says. "The blueberry and the chocolate chip are both really good."

"Ah, blueberry is my favorite," Harris says. "Maybe I'll get one. Do you have a favorite muffin?"

Courtney thinks about this for a moment.

"Actually, I never thought about it," Courtney says.

"Okay," Harris replies. "If you could only have one muffin for the rest of your life what would it be?"

This conversation may sound silly to you, but that's exactly the point. You don't have to talk about Italian cinema or feminist literature. Having a conversation about something like muffins is just as effective an opener because it can lead to other light conversation such as talking about which kinds of coffee they like the most. Also, the hypothetical question Harris poses to Courtney in the last line of their dialogue is great because it makes Courtney think for a moment. Harris is interested in her and he wants to know what she thinks. Consider how many days in your life go by without someone asking you what you think. Posing a silly hypothetical to someone plays against the lack of interest that goes on in society everyday. Hypothetical questions are fun. There are even books in your local bookstore full of hypothetical questions designed to be asked at dinner parties or on road trips. Try it out—it works. Let's look at one final example.

PROP EXAMPLE 6: TABLOIDS

Susan is at the supermarket. When she's done shopping, she approaches the check out area. At one station, she sees Charlie. He's handsome, so Susan chooses to stand on line behind Charlie, even though his line is a little bit longer than the others. She looks around for a prop with which to start a conversation and sees the tabloid, *The Globe.* Susan picks it up and laughs. She motions to Charlie holding the paper.

"Did you know Michael Jackson was kidnapped by aliens?" Susan asks.

"Hey, anything to keep him away from children," Charlie responds.

Susan laughs.

"Have you ever read one of these before?" Susan asks.

"Sure," Charlie says. "It's some of the most creative fiction on the market today."

Once again, you see how easy it is to start a conversation. In this scenario, both Susan and Charlie used humor to break the ice. Humorous props can be particularly effective. Humor is always a great lubricant to get you through the initial awkwardness that often plagues the beginnings of conversation. Being cute, clever, and funny helps people to drop their guard. In the next part, I'll demonstrate more techniques, in addition to humor, that you can use to keep your conversations going. However, before you can really charm them with your wit, remember, you have to start a conversation.

As practice, try to imagine yourself in the situations you find yourself in everyday. Try to think of props that you can use to stimulate an Indirect Approach. You'll get more spontaneous about what you use and how you use it as time goes by. Until that time, think about all of the different props you're likely to find in the places you frequent or places you know you'll be going. Come up with a few ways you could use them and keep them in your back pocket.

· 1 0 ·

Making the Right Impression

Whether you're blind dating, Internet dating, or meeting people about town, you will, at some point, end up in a conversation with another person you're interested in. Throughout the book thus far, you've read scenarios where people speak with one another. I've given you certain dialogues in order to give you an example of how easy it is to meet people and talk to them. Yet, out of necessity, the examples I've given you are short and often don't follow an entire conversation from beginning to end. If I did, this book would be far too long. In addition, it would be impossible for me to detail every possible way a conversation could go after an introduction. Therefore, this part of the book is dedicated to giving you some general guidelines about how to present yourself correctly in conversation.

Throughout my life and my career, I've stumbled on some universal truths when it comes to conversation. I don't like to use the word "rules" because it implies concrete laws that must never be broken. As always, there are exceptions to these truths, but generally these truths apply to most conversations between most people. We want these people to like us—that's the point. Know these truths and you'll master the art of conversation.

TRUTH 1: SEX STARTS AT HELLO

Let's face it, we're sexual creatures. We're also visual creatures—men generally more than women, but we all are. From the moment we start speaking with someone else they begin looking at us as a sexual being, even if subconsciously. Therefore, it's essential from the moment you make contact with someone else that you make the right impression and flirt the right way. Conversation and eye contact are both methods of flirting—as a matter of fact, almost everything you do when courting someone is flirting. Make them think about you in a sexy, playful, and flirtatious way and they'll begin to see you as many other things as well.

TRUTH 2: PEOPLE LIKE TO BE LOOKED IN THE EYE

Eye contact is essential to convey confidence. Confidence is sexy and makes people go weak in the knees. A famous acting teacher once said that "Your eyes are the windows to your soul." I believe this is true—you can tell a lot about someone by the look in their eyes. Next time you're talking to someone, study their eye movement, the depth in their eyes, and what their eyes are saying to you. Practice looking people in the eye, if you're not used to already doing so. Learn to be an actor. At the right time look away or down for dramatic effect—use your eyes to convey meaning and a message.

TRUTH 3: PEOPLE LIKE TO TALK ABOUT THEMSELVES

Everyone has a story. Every person, whether they're a farmer or a rock star, has a biography and their own opinions. People like to feel that they matter, that their life is worth something, that their opinions matter, and that others are interested in them. In conversation, it's better to listen than to talk. In a great conversation with another great communicator, you'll have the opportunity to do both because they'll listen and ask questions as well. Whenever you're in doubt, ask them about themselves. Ask them to elaborate when you're unclear of what they mean. Don't do this in an annoying way as if giving them the third degree. Do it in an, "I'm really interested in getting to know you more" type of way. Occasionally, throw in a comment of your own to break up the line of questioning, and make sure to remain attentive at all times.

TRUTH 4 : PEOPLE LIKE TO BE COMPLIMENTED

It could be the shoes on their feet or their intelligence, it doesn't matter—compliment them. People love to be complimented—even those who say they can't take a compliment. You don't want to over-compliment someone, so make sure to use it sporadically. Tell a woman she has pretty eyes or even cute ears. Tell her she has an interesting way of looking at politics, or that her jeans are sexy. Tell a man that he's got strong features or that he has a strong presence. Flatter him with a comment on his nice, broad shoulders. Whatever the case may be, try to come up with something. Everyone has qualities that stand to be admired.

Truth 5: Money Doesn't Talk

Most people know that it's inappropriate in the early stages of conversation to talk about the amount of money one makes. It sticks out like a dagger and can cut out any affection the person you're talking to might have for you. It's vain, narcissistic, and serves only to impress people in a superficial way. When the time is right, usually down the road, the topic will come up and you can tell the person about your finances. However, in the beginning, stay away from this topic at all costs. The type of person you want to meet would never be impressed with your financial revelations at the start anyway. If they are, then they'll probably disappear just as quickly as they arrived.

Truth 6: People Love to Hear Their Own Names

A person's name is music to their ears. I won't even begin to go into the psychological reason behind this—I just know it's true. When speaking to someone, use their name occasionally when talking. Just don't overuse it at the risk of becoming annoying.

Truth 7: Smile, Smile, Smile

Smiling conveys positive energy. We all like to be around positive energy. It makes people feel good—it lightens a mood—it's contagious.

Truth 8: People Love to Laugh

If you've got a good sense of humor, use it. The question is, how do you know if you have a good sense of humor? Most people believe they're funny, but sometimes they falter and their humor backfires on them. For instance, last week I was out with a group of guys when another guy whom I'd never met before, a friend of one of my friends, showed up. From the moment he got there he started making bad jokes and trying to do impersonations of celebrities that were simply awful—and that was with a bunch of men. I couldn't even imagine what he did on dates with women. Learn to be funny in a subtle way. Be sarcastic sometimes, self-deprecating at other times, and observational at others. Don't be the person practicing his routine for amateur night.

TRUTH 9: PEOPLE DON'T LIKE TO HEAR ABOUT YOUR EX

Generally, people don't like to hear about other people's ex-girlfriends or boyfriends—especially on a first encounter. However, on occasion, these topics do arise. When they do, the best way to handle the topic is to be positive. Try not to bash your ex because the person across from you will wonder what you will wind up saying about them should you two not work out. Say something like, "Yeah, he was actually a great guy, but we weren't connecting at the right levels." Or, "She was a terrific person, we just weren't right for each other." If asked to go into more detail, don't bash with harsh words like "He was an idiot," or "She was fat," or "He was a loser." Whether it's true or not, you'll come off as bitter and angry. Instead say, "He was a bright guy, but we had different interests," "We had very little chemistry," or "He had some career problems and needed to figure out where he was going in life." See the difference?

TRUTH 10: PEOPLE DON'T LIKE PRESSURE

Don't pressure people into talking to you or giving out their phone number—if they're interested, you won't have to. Occasionally, you can pressure someone into giving you their phone number, but from my experiences, 99 out of 100 times, it won't work out anyway. Ask once and if they say no, lightheartedly ask again. If it's still no, drop it and move on. There are others who will respond.

TRUTH 11: PEOPLE LIKE TO BE IMPRESSED IN SUBTLE WAYS

You're sitting and having a conversation with someone and you want so badly to reveal something about yourself—but you feel that if you just come out and say it, it'll come out wrong. Chances are, you're right. The best time to reveal something about yourself is when someone asks you a question. The best way to get someone to ask you questions about yourself is to pose the same question to them that you'd like to be asked. If they're at all interested in you, they'll respond with the same question. For instance, you're dying to tell someone that you are a doctor. While you also know that some people may regard your going on about it as an expression of self-importance, you also know that other women may see it as an attractive quality. Simply ask the other person what they do for a living and most of the time they will ask you what you do in return. If not, chances are this person could care less and it wouldn't matter if you were a senator—she's not going to respond.

·11·

Closing the Deal

Without the close, you don't get a number. If you don't get a number, you don't get a date. Without a date, you're back to square one—watching reality dating shows while eating Ben and Jerry's. There's an art form to closing a deal on a date just like there's an art form to closing a deal in business. However, surprisingly, some people have an easier time closing a multimillion dollar deal than when closing a deal to get a date.

Many of my clients have described closing the deal as one of the most anxiety-producing stages of the pickup. Perhaps it's because all of your work and creativity have built up to this final moment of truth—this climax—where you will find out if someone is receptive to getting to know you better. In this chapter, I give some things to consider when closing the deal and if you read carefully, the techniques will help release some anxiety.

However, before we go any further, I want to specifically address my female readers.

Ladies, throughout this book I've continually emphasized the need for you to break free of society's conventions and take control of your dating life. At this point, you should be ready to get proactive and seize upon any object of your desire. Yet, you must see it through to the end. Don't falter when you get to the close. Don't just sit around and wait until a man asks for your number. He may not ask. You do the asking. It will seem odd to you at first, but after a couple of tries, it'll become natural.

Many women feel that this is too aggressive and that it's threatening to a man's ego for a female to be so assertive. In response, I re-argue, that if a man is threatened by your assertiveness, he's not the man for you and the relationship would be doomed eventually anyway. Remember, we're no longer living in the 1950s. Women today are strong, wise, educated, and successful leaders in our society. Men who still expect women to cower in a corner waiting for Prince Charming are naïve and shallow. A strong, perceptive, and modern man will respect your assertiveness and be flattered that for once he didn't have to do all the work. He'll be flattered that you thought he was interesting enough to get to know better. He may even get turned on. I know—it's happened to me in the past and nothing could be sexier.

Many years ago, when I was in college, I was at a social event one evening with a group of friends. A young co-ed approached me from across the room and said, "You look like an interesting person. What's your name?" We talked for about twenty minutes, at which point she told me she had to go. However, before she did, she asked me if I'd like to meet her at the campus bohemian coffee shop on Sunday afternoon. I agreed and she asked for my number. I was blown away at how cool and confident she was. I was intrigued by her and couldn't wait to get to know her better. I didn't perceive her as either too aggressive or too easy— I perceived her as a woman who knew what she wanted and knew how to go after it. Follow her example and you'll take control of your dating destiny. Ask for what you want and you might just receive it. That's actually a lesson for women and men alike.

In business, we ask for what we want as plainly and clearly as we can. If we don't, it leaves ambiguity, and ambiguity in business deals is a recipe for a disastrous lawsuit. Although when dating, there's no litigation outside the occasional restraining order, we should still adhere to plain and clear logic. Too often in our social lives, shyness prevails, a conversation ends, and both parties walk away with one or both of them left hoping that they'll just happen to run into the other again. Life is all about seizing the opportunities that present themselves to you. It will do you no good if you make contact with someone and then blow it by not having the courage to take it a step further and ask for their phone number.

The first thing I want you to do when approaching the close is to take notice of what type of situation you're in and how you're going to handle it. Below is a list of questions I give to my clients to help them become more perceptive and aware of their challenge. I call these questions the Who, What, Where, Why, and How of Closing the Deal.

1. **Who are you going to ask?** What if you're in a group of people and you've been talking to all of them? If I had a

nickel for every time I was sitting and talking to a group of three or more pretty girls and couldn't decide which one to ask out, I'd be Donald Trump.

2. **What are you going to ask them?** Are you going to ask for a number or are you going to make the date right then and there? Usually, you go for the phone number, but occasionally you'll make the date right there and then. It's rare, and even if you do, you should get a phone number anyway so you can confirm plans.

3. **When in the conversation are you going to ask them?** For instance, you wouldn't ask someone for their phone number after you've just said hello. Granted, some people use this tactic, but its usually done by drunken college students in Cancun. As an adult, you have to find the appropriate time in your conversation to ask.

4. **Where are you going to actually pose the question?** For instance, you wouldn't ask out a business associate in front of other people in the office. You wouldn't ask out a waitress in front of the large group of people you were having dinner with. You'd want to take them aside or catch them alone where you can have a more intimate moment. You want the other person to be comfortable.

5. **Why are you asking them for their phone number?** Was your initial conversation strong and do you feel good about seeing this person again or are you doing it just for the sake of asking someone out? Either way, it's good practice and there's nothing wrong with asking for someone's phone number who you may not call or you don't know if you'll

call. Just because you've gotten someone's number doesn't mean you've made a commitment to them. You may change your mind later on and decide to call them or not to call them. However, at least you have the option.

6. **How are you going to ask them?** What will you say? What tone of voice will you use? Will you be sexy and confident? Will you be the Bumbler—the person who stutters and can't find the right words?

Use the Who, What, Where, Why, and How of Closing the Deal to ground you when you feel a conversation coming to a close and you're ready to make your move. Memorize them and have them at your disposal.

Now, below I'm going to go through several different deal-closing scenarios. As you read through them, casually keep in mind the Who, What, Where, Why, and How of Closing the Deal and see if you can figure out where each question comes into play. The scenarios are laid out in order of simplest to hardest.

SIMPLE SITUATION #1

The simplest situation you'll encounter is when you've just had a good conversation with a member of the opposite sex, neither one of you are in a rush, and the chemistry is apparent to both sides. For example, Howard and Andrea are sitting at a coffee shop on a sunny day. Howard, who made the original approach, wants this wonderful conversation to end on a high note. He realizes that he and Andrea have been talking for over an hour and he's ready to close the deal. How should he go about it? Very simply. He's going to ask her for her phone number and tell her exactly why he's asking.

"And that's how I became a doctor," Andrea says after telling her story to Howard.

"Wow! That's some story," Howard says. "Who would have ever thought you would choose your entire career off of accidentally sitting in a biology class rather than a philosophy class your freshman year of college?"

"I know," Andrea replies. "Funny how life works."

"Sure is," Howard says.

Howard stares at Andrea for a few seconds smiling. She smiles back. The moment is his. He must seize upon it or forever let this lovely creature out of his life.

"Andrea," Howard says, "I've had a great time talking to you. You seem to be an amazing person. I'd like to get to know you better. How about giving me your phone number and letting me take you out to dinner this Saturday."

"I'd love to," Andrea says. "Do you have a pen?"

"No," Howard replies. "But I've got my cell phone."

Let's examine how Howard went about closing the deal:

1. Howard makes great eye contact. As I said earlier, you should always look people in the eye. It's hypnotic. Don't stare at people like you're going to kill them. Look at them confidently, like you're examining them, and you're inviting them into your mind through your eyes.

2. Howard compliments Andrea before he asks her out. He tells her he's had a great time talking to her and that she's an "amazing" person. In fact, she's so amazing, Howard

would like to get to know her better. Barring Andrea having other commitments, she really has no reason to say no to Howard. They've just had a great conversation, she told him her life story, and they're flirting with their eyes—it's obvious chemistry. I can't think of any reason why Andrea wouldn't be excited to give Howard her phone number—even if at first she doesn't find Howard the most handsome gentleman around.

As I said earlier in this book, men, you don't have to look like a movie star for women to like you. However, you do have to possess some sex appeal. Sex appeal comes from good grooming, dressing well, and being cool, calm, and confident. It means, you know what you want and you put it out there in a nonthreatening way. Look a woman in the eyes, tell her she's beautiful, interesting and you want to take her out. It's easier than you think.

The problems that many men have is that they either don't have the guts to say what they want or they don't do it the right way. You ladies out there reading know exactly what I'm talking about. How many times have you been approached by men who you weren't initially attracted to, who if they'd simply asked you out in the right way, you would have gone out with them? Men, I challenge you. For every time you think you've been shot down for the way you look, I will show you ten ugly guys that are either in relationships or date attractive women, because they have confidence and they know the way into a woman's heart.

3. Howard asked Andrea for her phone number and suggested the day he wanted to see her. Again, like I've said

before, women like men who know what they're doing. Never show up at a woman's door and say, "So, what do you want to do tonight?" That's for when you're married and are both indecisive.

Whether you're a man or a woman, when you're courting, have your plans laid out beforehand. Of course, always have a game plan B. For instance, if you make reservations for a steak house and later find out your date is a vegetarian, don't force them to go to the steak house. In the previous scenario, Howard asked Andrea out for Saturday night—not for sometime. He could have asked for sometime, and that probably would have worked for him. However, this way, if she doesn't object, he's got a definite date for that Saturday. If she isn't free on Saturday evening, then he could say, "How about Friday?"—game plan B. If she's also busy Friday, he could ask for the following Tuesday. The point is, as often as possible, try to be the decisive one. The world is full of people who have no direction, no plan, and who can't make decisions, which can be really annoying. Don't be one of them.

4. It would have been too easy if Howard had a pen on him. I threw the cell phone into the scenario so you'll never use the fact that you don't have a pen handy as an excuse not to ask for a number. Here, Howard had his cell phone which, these days, most of us have. And if you have one, you also know you can just type in somebody's number.

However, let's say Howard didn't have his cell phone handy or even a pen. Then what? Howard could have gone inside the coffee shop and asked the person behind the register for a pen, grabbed a napkin, and headed back outside. You're never far from a pen. Businesses are everywhere and they all have pens. If you're not in a city, use bark. No bark? Use lipstick. It's no excuse to not get someone's number because you don't have a pen handy. Think creatively!

SIMPLE SITUATION #2

The prior scenario entailed a conversation between Howard and Andrea that existed over the period of at least an hour. So, how do you close the deal when you haven't been talking as long? What do you do in a brief encounter? Remember, you don't have to have an hour-long conversation like Howard and Andrea to get a number. Most of the time, you won't. The following scenario is one that was relayed to me by a client of mine named Doug.

One day, Doug and his friend Ken were out walking together when Ken decided to go to his hair salon and get a haircut. While Doug was waiting for Ken in the front of the salon, he noticed a beautiful brunette sitting in the waiting area. Doug noticed she was looking at one of those hairstyle picture albums—or as we say, a prop.

"See anything good in there?" Doug asked the woman.

The woman turned the photo album toward Doug and showed him a picture of a woman with a crew cut. Doug winced.

"I don't think it's you," Doug said. "Here, let me take a stab at it."

Doug reached for the book and the woman handed it to him. He flipped through a couple of pages and then turned it over to show a picture of a woman with a green mohawk.

"I think that's more your style," Doug said.

The woman laughed.

"You think so, do you?" she said in a thick accent.

"Oh, I like your accent," Doug said. "Where are you from?"

"South Africa," the woman said.

"What part?" Doug asked.

"Cape Town," the woman replied.

"I've heard it's beautiful there," Doug said. "Always wanted to go. Can I stay at your house?"

"Perhaps," the woman said. "Although I think my parents turned my old bedroom into a closet. Do you mind sleeping in a closet?"

Doug laughed.

"What's your name?" Doug asked.

"Cynthia," the woman replied.

"I'm Doug," he said.

Doug shook her hand, but just as he did, Cynthia's hairdresser called her to go get her hair washed.

"Well, Doug, it was nice meeting you," Cynthia said. "I have to go get my crew cut now."

"Wait," Doug said. "You have to give me your phone number first. I want to hear about growing up in South Africa."

Cynthia smiled.

"Okay," she said. "Let me write it down."

How long did they talk? Maybe two minutes—tops. Yet, in that two minutes Doug was able to make Cynthia laugh, get her name, where she was from, make her laugh again, and get her phone number. He acted quickly and confidently and as a result, closed the deal. It's really that easy. Doug made her feel comfortable by his relaxed, confident conversation. Cynthia also felt comfortable because Doug was in a place familiar to her—the salon she frequents.

When people meet other people in places that are familiar to them, it's almost as if someone introduced them. Subconsciously, Cynthia thinks that he must be safe, since he goes to the same salon. Crazy, right? The salon is like an intermediary. Remember, you don't have to have an hour conversation—you just have to be confident in your close.

MORE DIFFICULT SITUATION #1

The following scenario is an example of what to do when you're in a mad rush to close the deal.

One weekday, in the early 1990s, I was on a subway in Manhattan. I boarded the subway at 34th Street and was headed to 96th Street. At 51st Street, a woman got on the train who I found desirable. I quickly struck up a conversation with her and she informed me she was getting off at 86th Street. The ride between 51st Street and 86th Street takes all of five minutes on a slow day. Here is how I skillfully got her number as we quickly approached her stop.

"Listen, I know your stop is coming up in a few seconds and we haven't talked long, but I'd really like to continue this conversation," I said. "How about giving me your cell phone number and I'll call you as soon as I get off at 96th Street?"

"I don't know," she said playfully.

"I'll make a deal with you," I said. "If I call and you don't like me, you can hang up the phone without even saying goodbye."

"Well, with an offer like that, how can I refuse?" she said. "Get your cell phone ready."

Why would she give her number to a complete stranger she talked to for a minute on a subway during rush hour? After all, she didn't know if I was a psychopath—she met me on a train in New York. It was all in my delivery and how I presented myself. I came across as a funny, confident guy who she had a brief encounter with. Also, by asking explicitly for her cell phone number, she knew that even if I was a psychopath, I would never be able to stalk her—another benefit of the cell phone.

Needless to say, when I got off the subway at 96th Street, I immediately called her, we spoke for ten minutes, and we went on a date that weekend.

MOST DIFFICULT SITUATION: #1

Quite possibly the most difficult situation you'll encounter is when you have an encounter with not one but several people, and you want to get the phone number of just one of them. Let's use Howard and Andrea again from the coffee shop in Simple Situation #1. Suppose, it was Andrea who wanted to get Howard's number, yet, Howard wasn't alone—he was with a group of friends. This can be an intimidating situation because all eyes will be on Andrea and Howard if she asks Howard for his phone number. However, there's a simple way for Andrea to get Howard's number without making a big production. Check out the following example:

Andrea's sitting around a table with Howard and his four college friends. They're all laughing and having a good time. Andrea looks at her watch and sees that if she doesn't leave, she will be late for an appointment.

"It's 4:00," Andrea says, looking at her watch. "I have an appointment at 4:15. I guess I better get going. It was nice meeting you all."

"It was nice meeting you too," they all say in unison.

Andrea looks at Howard.

"You know, you should give me your number," Andrea says. "We could all meet up again some time and tell some more dating war stories."

"Yeah, sounds good," they say in agreement.

That should do the trick. When Andrea asked for the number she looked directly at Howard. Howard, unless he is completely dim-witted, will get the picture. If he doesn't get the picture, Andrea can simply ask Howard for his number and because Andrea said that she wanted get together with everyone, it won't be uncomfortable. However, nine out of ten times a man will pick up on this and give you his number. The same would be the case if it was a man asking for a woman's number who was surrounded by her friends. It's all about who you ask and how you ask them. Speak with your eyes. Focus your confidence on the object of your desire. Body language works. Trust in it.

The most important thing to take from this part of the book is the Who, What, Where, Why, and How of Closing the Deal. Always remember to have confidence when closing the deal. Focus your attention on that person, be cool, and don't let brief encounters cause you to allow a potential date to get away. Never let them smell fake fear.

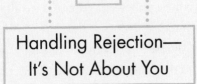

Handling Rejection— It's Not About You

If you get someone's number, that's great. If you don't, that's great, too. Hey, you went for it. That's the most important thing. Remember, you went the distance like Rocky. Now, you've got to prepare for the sequel. Don't let ruminating thoughts of rejection haunt you. You're putting this into your mind as a successful experience. You didn't die. It didn't end up in *The New York Times* or even the local paper. Getting rejected says nothing about you as a person.

People have all kinds of reasons for not wanting to give out their phone number. They may be in a relationship, they may have just gotten out of a relationship, they may be dating someone they like and they think it could turn into a relationship. It could also be that they simply aren't attracted to you. You will never really know their reasons, so why bother torturing yourself trying to figure it out? Let me tell you a story about a client of my named George.

When George was a teenager he was unsuccessful with girls. He used to sit around and watch his friends always get the girls he wanted to date. As a young guy, this was frustrating for George—especially during those pubescent years. As we all know, there are only two things important during those years—school and adolescent romance. Those years can be very confusing for young people and a lot of the times they become the victims of their own innocence. George was a perfect example—his first negative experience with women haunted him for years.

In the sixth grade, George had a Friday night birthday party. On one side of the party several of George's guy friends were hooking up with the cute girls in his class. George desperately wanted to be a part of that—he'd never even kissed a girl, but he was ready to give it a go like his friends. His only goal became finding a girl, asking her to be his girlfriend, and joining the kissing fest. Over the course of the evening, George approached three different girls and asked them if they wanted to be his girlfriend. Unfortunately, despite it being George's birthday, none said yes. It was a frustrating, disappointing, and humiliating experience for George. Naturally, he took it personally, and let it affect him for years to come. His confidence was low to begin with—now it was in the toilet.

Several years passed and George still had yet to have a physical encounter with a girl. He desperately wanted a girl's affection, but couldn't muster the confidence to approach another girl for fear of being humiliated once again. It wasn't until the summer of his sophomore year of high school that George finally began to rebuild the damage that had been done to him five years earlier. That summer, George was at a camp—a place where no one knew him or of his past experiences. One day, his camp unit got on a bus to go on a day trip. George, being the funny guy he was, suddenly became the center of attention. Everyone crowded around him as he told stories and made jokes. Then, from across the bus, a pretty young sixteen-year-old girl looked at George in a way that conveyed her romantic interest. Feeling on top of the world being in his new surroundings, George stuck up a conversation with the girl. By the end of the day, George and the girl were at the back of the bus making out, and they continued to date all summer long.

After that encounter, George wondered what he'd been fearful of all those years. Why had he let one bad night of experiences with girls when he was in the sixth grade affect him for five years? George had tasted success and he wanted more of it. His confidence grew and he promised himself never to let a rejection get him down again. George never knew why those girls at his party turned him down, but for years he figured it was because he was geeky. Perhaps he was right, perhaps those girls did think of him as a geek back then. Yet, the fact is, another girl—the camp girl—never saw him as a geek at all. Remember, different strokes for different folks. Never let a rejection get you down. If you think you did something wrong during the encounter to turn the other person off, be honest with yourself. Analyze it, correct it, and get back out there. If not, chalk it up to personal taste and move on. Don't let moments pass you by. You'll regret it—I did.

For most of my adult life, I've been a confident person.

Yet, like many young people, I had my occasional lapses of confidence, and to this day, I tell the following story to my clients to emphasize the need for them to seize the day.

When I was in college, I had the biggest crush on a girl named Wendy James. She was beautiful, popular, bright, and sophisticated. I know, it's starting to sound like a teen movie—just wait. When I first saw Wendy my freshman year of college, I immediately put her in a Fantasy Box. To me, she was unattainable. I put her on such a pedestal that over the next couple of years, I could barely speak a word to her other than the occasional hello. I was so nervous around her, it was as if I had peanut butter and sawdust on my tongue. So, what did your Dating Guru do instead of walking right up to Wendy and asking her on a date? I asked out her friends. All of them. I'm not kidding—I really did—as if that was the way into her heart. One of her friends, Jordan, I actually ended up dating on a regular basis. Yet, the whole time while I was with Jordan, I was thinking about Wendy. I'm embarrassed to admit this—but I even asked Jordan once while we were dating if she thought Wendy would go out with me. Hey, I was a kid! Despite this ridiculous question, Jordan and I continued to date for about four months.

The next semester of school, I found myself in a literature class with Wendy. For the first two months of class, I had no idea what was going on in that class because I spent the entire time ogling Wendy. Finally, one day, I saw Wendy pack up her books in the middle of class and head for the door. Something overcame me and I followed her out of the lecture hall.

When I walked out of the class, I didn't see her. I walked to the exit of the building, stepped outside, and saw her heading down the steps. It was a beautiful spring day, the flowers were starting to bloom, and the sky was cloudless and blue. She was all alone—I had her to myself. There was one month left of school before we graduated. It had to be then.

"Wendy," I called out.

Wendy gracefully turned around, her hair blowing in the light breeze. She pulled it back from her sparkling emerald eyes.

"Hey, David," she said. "How are you?"

A lump formed in my throat—she was actually asking me how I was. I began to sweat underneath my shirt.

"Boring class, huh?" was all I managed to squeak out.

"So boring," she said. "I had to get out of there. Are you leaving too?"

Almost four years of being afraid of rejection was standing between Wendy and me. "David," I said to myself. "Just do it, already."

"No," I said. "I actually, well, I came outside to ask you if you were busy this week. Do you want to have dinner with me?"

I couldn't believe the words finally left my mouth. Four years they'd been locked inside of me. Now, there they were, floating between my mouth and her adorable little ears. I prayed for her to say yes.

"That's so sweet," she said. "But I've been dating someone for three months now—it's getting kind of serious. You should've asked me out last semester. I would've said yes."

I was speechless. Last semester I was dating her friend Jordan. I wanted to crawl into a hole. I wanted to jump off a building. I wanted to kick myself—rather, I wanted to stand behind a horse and let it kick me. However, none of that would've eased the pain.

The damage had been done. Suddenly, it became so clear—I'd missed out on Wendy because I'd let a fear of rejection control me. There was nothing I could do at that point but accept the situation, learn from my mistake, and move on. I stood up straight and smiled at her.

"Good for you," I said. "I hope it works out."

"Thanks," she said smiling back. "Maybe I'll see you out this Friday at one of the bars."

"I hope," I said. And with that, she turned away, walked down the path, and out of sight.

Many of you have stories like this one and many of you have heard stories like it. However, this is my story and it had a profound impact on my life. After that experience, I resolved never to let fear of rejection get between me and what I wanted again. Whether it was in my social life or in my career, from that day forward I controlled my fear, put it in perspective, and went after what I wanted—in spite of possible rejection. Perhaps that moment had a more profound impact on me than I even realize. Perhaps it was why I chose to help people for a living. Don't let opportunities pass you by because you fear rejection. Go after what you want. At the very least, if you don't succeed, you'll have closure.

Making the Phone Call

Unlike other dating coaches, I firmly believe that there are no hard-and-fast rules governing when to call someone for a date. Forget about the three-day grace period—use the momentum of an enjoyable conversation to motivate you. However, never throw common sense by the wayside. For instance, you shouldn't call someone the same day you get their number, and you shouldn't call someone too late at night or too early in the morning.

Calling someone the same day, unless there's good reason, looks desperate and anxious. Yet, there's nothing wrong with calling someone the day after you've met them. Calling the next day gives a person just enough time to digest your meeting, yet, at the same time, isn't so far off that you'll need to explain to them who you are. At most, all you'll have to do is say, "Hi, John, it's Cindy Jones, we met yesterday at the concert."

Waiting more than three days to call someone could potentially turn someone off—they may think that you're flaky or trying to play the delayed calling game so often talked about in the dating world and in movies like *Swingers*. In short, call somewhere between one to three days after your initial meeting and reintroduce yourself by quickly reminding the person who you are and where you met.

Next, try not to call too late at night or too early in the morning. Again, common sense should tell you that people are too groggy and rushed in the morning, and too tired and exhausted late at night to have any form of stimulating conversation. Also, you run the risk of waking them out of a cold sleep—not a good way to start off your courting. Instead, in my experience both personally and with clients, the best time I've found to call someone is between 9:30 and 10:00 at night—when they're finally relaxing.

Remember, most of us work long, hard days. Then after work, many of us run errands, go to the gym, have dinner, and finally, finish the day by watching our favorite television shows. Most Americans, between the hours of 9:30 and 10:00 at night, have had a chance to do these things, are in their pajamas, and vegetating in front of the television, or reading a book. By calling at this time, you've given the person a chance to unwind from the fast-paced insanity of their daily life and they'll be much more willing to relax on the phone with you—or, shall I say, become intimate. In addition, from a psychological perspective, it's also a time of the day when single people realize they're alone. Your voice will be welcomed, soothing, and comforting, and will have the subconscious effect of them no longer feeling alone. The best part—your voice will be one of the last things they hear before drifting off to sleep. Say the right things and you may even get them to dream about you.

In the blind-dating chapter of this book, I gave some tips on the right things to say on that first phone call. Again, I don't believe in any rules. I've had first-call conversations with women that have lasted three hours and I've had calls that have lasted three minutes. At times, I've become extremely intimate with someone on the phone, and at others, I've talked just enough to set up a date. It's up to you to use your common sense to gauge whether the other person is up for a long talk. Never cut off a great conversation for the sake of simply cutting it off. Yet, never try to force someone to talk when you're getting a vibe that they don't want to talk at that point in time. Listen to their voice, listen to the way they respond to your questions or to what you're saying, and pay attention to whether they're paying attention. Remember, always be aware.

For many people, that first phone call can be an intimidating experience. Occasionally, I get clients who tell me they get anxious that they won't be able to keep the conversation flowing—they don't know the person well enough. Sometimes, subsequent to them setting up a date, they even fake having to get off the phone quickly to ease their anxiety. If you have this anxiety problem, I suggest sitting down at your kitchen table just before you call the person and answering the following questions on a pad:

1. Where did I meet this person?

2. How did I meet this person?

3. What did I learn about this person by the way they dressed and carried themselves?

4. What did I learn about this person during my conversation?

   a. Where is this person originally from?

   b. Where do they live now?

   c. What is their career?

   d. Where did they go to college?

   e. Did I find out about their family?

   f. What kind of movies, music, television shows, and books do they like?

   g. Where do they like to travel, where have they traveled, where would they like to travel?

5. What do I have in common with this person?

6. What do I not have in common with this person?

7. What is my game plan A and game plan B for the date I'm going to ask them on? Will I pick them up or will I meet them there?

When you make the phone call, have the answers to these questions in front of you and refer to them as necessary. If you didn't get an answer to some of these questions when you first met the person, ask them when you're on the phone. Of course, skillfully transition into these questions—don't just dial the number and say, "Hi, this is David. Where did you go to school?" Build upon what you already know of the person or simply find out new and interesting facts about their lives. Cleverly let them know a little about your life and what you're like. Try not to force questions, just let the conversations unravel as naturally as possible. If you feel a lull coming on say, "Hey, I was just curious, where are you from originally?" When they answer, you'll have a whole new topic to explore. Remember how earlier I discussed the significance of using Portal Words to keep a conversation fresh? Pick up on Portal Words to assist you in diving into a whole new area of conversation.

The last thing I want to address is tone of voice. The tone in which you speak to someone should always be day and time appropriate. Don't let your anxiety or the fact that you're excited to talk to this person take over. Not many people on a weekday evening want to hear someone on the other end of the phone that sounds like they've just had their first cup of coffee for the day. Relax with them, unwind with them, calm and soothe them, talk with them—not at them, be playful, be humorous, and be a little sexy and flirtatious when the time is right. Use your common sense. As in all conversation, listen carefully to what the other person is saying. Most importantly, leave the other person wanting more.

conclusion

Congratulations on completing this book. I hope that I've delivered on my promise and you've garnered some insight into what it takes to meet new people to date, specifically, how your mindset and physical appearance can affect you in both positive and negative ways, where to go to find new single people, and once you find them, how to go about starting a conversation with them, maintaining it, and then finally, getting a date.

Meeting new people to date is easy and fun, and can open up your entire world if you treat it as a journey rather than a chore. Remember, you're in no rush. Take your time, build up your skills, enjoy the journey, and eventually, you, like all of my clients, will end up in healthy relationships. Digesting what I've taught in this book is the first step to finding those healthy relationships and it's a step that can't be skipped. Master the skills, learn from the anecdotes, be proactive, and soon, you'll start to see the results. As you apply what you've learned and let it become a part of you, you'll never again let anxiety, fear, or your past negative experiences stop you from going after what you want. You are in the present and the present holds invigorating, passion-filled, exciting experiences for you. But remember, they won't just fall into your lap. *You* have to seize the experiences that *you* want.

If you feel this book has helped you and you want to learn even more, I highly recommend you explore my Websites **www.davidwygant.com** and **www.alwaystalktostrangers.com**. On my Websites, you'll be able to find information on my latest press appearances and my other products, such as my four-CD series, *Dating Steps*, which builds upon what I've started in this book. If you want more individualized attention, I am also available for one-on-one intensive personal coaching, both domestically and abroad.

Until then, I'd like to thank you for allowing me to share my knowledge with you and I want to wish you all the best as you venture back into the dating world.